Th
Co₁

-

LANREATH

----

by
Tony Latham

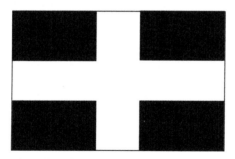

The Cornish flag, said to be the flag of St Piran who was the patron saint of tin miners. Tradition is that tin melted out of a stone on St Piran's fire, and formed a cross. The white represents tin and the black being the tin ore.

First published in the United Kingdom in 2015 by
The Choir Press

ISBN 978-1-910864-19-7

Acknowledgement is given to the authors of many books used as a source of historical information during the writing of this book, as well as information posted on the Internet. I have tried as much as possible to look at Cornwall in general, but to see it through the eyes of a single village in which I used to live - Lanreath.

As I am not a historian, I have written the book for those who want to know more about this wonderful county in an enjoyable way, whether a visitor or resident, and not as a historical reference source.

Main sources of information:

A History of Cornwall: by F E Halliday
Children's History of Cornwall: by Peggy Burns
Freedom of the Parish: by Geoffrey Grigson
Cornwall and the Cross: by Nicholas Orme
Lostwithiel 1644: by Stephen Ede-Borrett
The History of Polperro: by Jonathan Couch
Cornwall: by Craig Weatherhill
Mysterious Cornwall: by Rupert Matthews
Cornwall's History: by Philip Payton
St Marnarch's Church, Lanreath: by Rosemary Pollock
The Grylls of Lanreath: by Richard Grylls
The Giant's Hedge/Lanreath School: Lanreath WI

My very grateful thanks to all those who proof-read my manuscript, corrected errors and added value. In particular, Richard Grylls, Rosemary Pollock, and especially my son, James.

The cover painting depicting the tale of the 'Headless Horses' (see page 84-85) was by Geoff Herickx, a former church minister, professional artist, and longtime friend. The original canvas measures 4ft x3ft. Smaller copies on canvas may be purchased from the author on request.

For
Katie and James

Tony Latham is a media specialist working with a variety of materials, especially film. Uniquely for media production consultants, he not only writes, films, edits and narrates the commentary for most of his films, but writes drama stories for radio in developing countries.

Tony started his overseas career as a volunteer (VSO) in Africa, after working for the BBC producing news film for many years. This led to a consultancy appointment with the British government for three years based in Africa, and then employment as a UNESCO consultant for another three years. Following this, Tony returned to the UK to become Director of Overseas Film Production and a board member of a UK company, during which time he was responsible for making over 100 films in Africa, funded mainly by the World Bank, EU and the Nigerian River Basin and Rural Development Authority. He became an independent consultant and filmmaker in 1983, working on projects funded by the World Bank, Asian and African Development Banks, EU, DFID, Unido, IFAD, The Ford Foundation, ICI Agrochemicals, private companies and organizations, and a variety of overseas governments. Tony officially retired in 2011, leaving him time to indulge his passion for writing, and thus this book.

Tony has worked in many countries of the world, including Bangladesh, Bhutan, Brazil, Cameroon, Dominica, Egypt, Ethiopia, Germany, Ghana, India, Ivory Coast, Jamaica, Kenya, Liberia, Namibia, Nepal, Nigeria, Pakistan, Philippines, Rwanda, Spain, St Vincents and the Grenadines, Tanzania, Thailand, The Gambia, Tonga, Uganda, USA, Vanuatu, Yemen where the above picture overlooking the Old City was taken, and Zambia.

Constructive comments to add value to this book are most welcome,

tony.latham95@gmail.com

Contents

The oldest person in Lanreath on the day of the Queen's Diamond Jubilee was Ida Pollock, aged 104, and the youngest, Mia Nicole Rollings born on 21st September 2010

Introduction:

Lanreath

Lanreath is a Cornish village that punches well above its weight, and as a local radio presenter Michael Taylor stated on May Day 2008, "*Is the envy of every other village in Cornwall for what it has achieved.*" Indeed, from a low point at the beginning of the new millennium, until the time of the Queen's Diamond Jubilee on 2 June 2012, the village boasted a number of success stories.

At the heart of Lanreath is a Millennium building, set within the village green, and the focus of many annual activities. Above, converted from a former toilet block in the pub car park, is the village shop and Post Office, run successfully by an elected village committee and supporting a part time manageress and almost 20 volunteers.

Also in the centre of the village is the famous Punch Bowl Inn, licensed in 1620 to sell the newly imported drink recipe from India called *Panch*. It was rescued from closure by a local resident family in 2007, but unfortunately closed again on May Day 2012, and at the time of writing nobody is sure if it will open again.

The oldest buildings at the time of the Jubilee are in this part of the village and include the Cob Cottages, and cottages running each side of the Punch Bowl Inn, some in cob, a mixture of sub-soil and straw, and some rebuilt or replaced.

The newest houses being built at the time of the Jubilee can be found at the top of the village, two on the site of the former village school, and eleven others just below. In addition, a small development by a local resident will add eighteen houses to the village, ensuring growth in the years to come.

The oldest resident at the time of the Jubilee was the author Ida Pollock, who reached 104 in 2012. Married to the glamorous soldier and publisher Major Hugh Pollock, the former husband of Enid Blyton, Ida used nine pen-names, had five publishers, and over a million readers worldwide. Ida died on the 3rd December 2013.

The youngest resident at the time of the Jubilee was Mia Nicole Rollings, born on 21st September 2010 to Lydia and John.

The Lanreath Village Hall is the venue for a number of events throughout the year, used by the hall committee itself, the Rally Social Club, the Lanreath Football Club, the Parochial Church Council, the

9

Ladybirds toddlers' group, the Lanreath Amenities Group and the parish council. Events range from musical evenings, bingo nights, firework displays, May Day celebrations, safari suppers, badminton, long-mat bowls, toddlers' meetings and ad-hoc events throughout the year. The village has an informative newsletter distributed to all residents, and its own website – www.lanreath.com

In 2011, the Lanreath Amenities Group of seven people won the Queen's Diamond Jubilee award for voluntary service, one of just 15 in the whole of South-west of England.

The Lanreath Amenities Group

So popular was the village, that in 2007 *BBC Two* made a one-hour documentary on the village called *Power to the People*, that praised the fighting spirit of the residents and the achievements they had made. Mainly: the opening of the pub, village shop and post office, albeit unfortunately the school was closed after 179-years of teaching generations of children.

Lanreath has a history that goes back thousands of years, maybe to the Bronze Age, as a tomb and artefacts have been found on the border of the parish. Thus, people could have roamed the surrounding hills around the village 4,000-years ago and would have drunk from springs that still run through Lanreath today.

QUEEN'S DIAMOND JUBILEE

Bronze Age stone circle at Duloe - the smallest in Cornwall (2000 BC)

Above: Axe-head mould, maybe Bronze Age
Right: Various carved pieces of flint stone
(all found at Beara farm, Lanreath)

Bronze Age tomb - found in a field on the edge of Lanreath village

Chapter One:

The Bronze and Iron Age Celts - 2000 BC to AD 43

Visible but unseen, Bury Down rises from a ridge overlooking Lanreath village in Cornwall, yet only a handful of residents would be aware of this Iron Age settlement, let alone have visited one of the oldest historical sites in the parish. But thousands of years before Bury Down was settled, Neolithic man arrived on the west coast of England in waves from the Mediterranean, travelling in primitive boats from across the channel, which was much narrower than it is today. Our Cornish Mediterranean ancestor-settlers can be identified by their traditions, ultimately going back to their Middle East ancestors by the way they buried their dead in mausoleum tombs. These can still be seen today in Cornwall, constructed of gigantic slabs of granite, many not far from Lanreath.

Bury Down hill fort, Lanreath   *Trethevy Quoit*

Pawton Quoit near Wadebridge, with its 14.6 tonne capstone, is the heaviest in Cornwall. Nearby is Trethevy Quoit on the southern edge of Bodmin Moor – the word Quoit meaning capstone.

Our story relating to Cornwall in general and Lanreath in particular starts around the year 2000 BC, when Bronze, and later Iron Age Celtic immigrants were living across Europe, including England and Cornwall. This was the age of metal, with bronze then iron being used for weaponry, and for domestic purposes.

Around 500 BC to AD 1, the Cornish Celts built hill forts with banks, ramparts and ditches for protection. Bury Down is a fine example of a Celtic hill fort. Many roundhouses would have been built inside, with conical-shaped and thatched roofs, a fireplace in the centre, and wattle screens separating different areas.

Celtic roundhouse

Like several Cornish Iron Age hill forts, Bury Down doesn't stand on the hilltop, but on the west-facing slope, seven metres below the summit. Oval in shape, it consists of two widely spaced ramparts and ditches with overall diameters of 195m by 170m. The inner of the two ramparts reach an impressive 4.3m. The entrance faces west, with the eastern side being of questionable origin.

In addition to the many springs and streams that are a feature in the Lanreath area, one in particular stands out. This is a spring-fed pond that lies at the very highest point on Bury Down. Located slightly higher than the Iron Age settlement, it's perfectly positioned to supply running water to those living within the ramparts of the hill fort.

The language of these Lanreath Celts, as in most of Cornwall and Wales, will have been Brythonic - the predecessor of Cornish. The Celts inhabited vast areas, including Scotland, Wales and Cornwall, which extended into modern Devon and Somerset and across into Brittany. The Cornish Celts were, strictly speaking, *Britons* in language and culture, more closely linked to their French cousins in Brittany and other parts of France. Thus, in later centuries *Great* Britain was used, to refer to all of the United Kingdom.

Gaulish, the language of the Gauls, who resided then in what is now France, was almost indistinguishable from Brythonic. Indeed, the Iron Age Cornish Celts traded internationally because of their common language, enabling cross-channel trade to flourish.

Cornwall's first known tourist was Pytheas of Massilia (Marseilles), a Greek scribe who visited on a trading ship in 325 BC.

Writing up his exploits in detail, he called the Cornish *"Hospitable and civilized,"* as he travelled visiting the sites of the tin mining industry. Finally, he headed north by sea and circumnavigated

Bury Down Iron Age settlement - Lanreath

the British islands before returning to his home country.

The Cornish Celts were relatively small in stature and a peace-loving people. Thus, they needed defensive positions to protect their precious metal assets from other warrior-group immigrants who were bigger, stronger, and had superior weapons.

Most importantly, the Celts learned how to process Cornwall's metals, such as tin, found in abundance in the gravel, silt, clay and sand of the surrounding area, including east Cornwall on Bodmin Moor, and maybe lead and silver from Herodsfoot - formally within Lanreath parish. Some gold was also mined in Cornwall.

The Celts living in Cornwall learnt not only to extract tin ore from the ground, but to smelt it at low temperatures into pure tin. They then beat the metal into an ingot shaped like a knucklebone, and sold this for exporting to Europe. They also mixed some of the tin with

15

Spring at Bury Down

copper to form bronze, and created beautiful decorated objects such as shields, swords and jewellery. Some they traded for the commodities they couldn't produce themselves.

Copper was not found in Cornwall in any great quantity, but was mined in abundance in Ireland. As tin was not mined in Ireland, a mutually beneficial trade was established. This involved Irish merchants sailing to the north Cornwall coast and landing in the quiet Camel estuary at Padstow. Gold was also mined in Ireland and traded for Cornish tin. *Gold lunulae*, necklaces in the form of crescents, have been found in the Padstow area that date from this time. After arriving, they would trade their copper for Cornish tin, and return to Ireland – this saved them having to navigate the choppy waters around Land's End to trade directly with Europe. The Cornish then took the copper overland to Fowey, and together with their own tin, crossed the channel to sell and trade in Europe. At one time, Cornwall was the largest source of tin in the world. Tin was a rare metal in Europe, and together with the knowledge to produce bronze, Cornwall was at the front of this early, cross channel trade.

According to Pytheas, the 4th century Greek scribe, it is recorded in addition that on the island of *Iktus*, probably St Michael's mount, that at low tide the land between the island and the mainland dries out, as it still does today, and they can take the tin over in their wagons in large quantities. It has also been suggested that Iktus could have been Looe island. Merchants bought tin from the Cornish and carried it from there across the Strait of Galatia, now known as the English channel, and finally made their way through Gaul for some thirty days, bringing the goods on horseback to the mouth of the Rhone.

In the years before the birth of Christ, a tribe called the Belgae had established themselves in eastern Kent. They were from Celtic stock that had inter-married with barbaric German tribes. From their British base they actively supported their north-east Gaul kinsmen's resistance in what is now present day France, against the Romans, and that was the reason imperial Rome invaded Britain in 55 BC. When Caesar landed with a fighting force of ten-thousand men near Deal in August of 55 BC. they may have thought that this mist-shrouded island would be an easy target. However, it was the battle tactics of the Belgae charioteers fighting alongside the British that won the day, and eventually beat the Romans back. The following year, a second invasion was more successful for the Romans. After victory, a peace deal was agreed between Rome and Britain, and Caesar left to fight the Gauls in France. It was to be another 100-years before the Romans invaded Britain again.

St Michael's Mount at low tide

17

Roman milestone at St Materiana's church, Tintagel

Chapter Two:

Roman Period - AD 43 to AD 410

Following the two Roman invasions of 55 BC and 54 BC, the Belgae ceased their support for their Gaul kinsmen in France, in exchange for the Romans not occupying Britain. This left the Belgae free to push out of their base in Kent and rule more of Britain as far as central Devon. Although this had little direct impact on Cornwall, with Gaul now under Roman occupation, exports of tin ceased. When the Belgae king died in about AD 40, Britain began to fall apart, offering a perfect opportunity for another Roman invasion.

In AD 43 Claudius dispatched a powerful army which rapidly overran the Belgae territory. The Romans set up a camp in what was to become Exeter in about AD 50. Over the next few years they pushed west into Wales, and north, but being unable to defeat the Caledonian Picts, built Hadrian's wall to seal off Scotland.

As the Romans had acquired tin from Spain, there was little point in occupying Cornwall with legions of men. They left it mainly to Roman merchants and administrators to establish forts in places such as Nanstallon near Bodmin, Restormel just north of Lostwithiel, and Calstock near Callington. Restormel fort is thought to have been occupied for 300 years by the Romans, becoming an administrative centre for the extraction of iron. The fort itself sits on an iron lode, and iron slag can still be found on the site. Also, due to their contact with the Mediterranean, the Cornish were considered more civilised and peaceful than the rest of Britain. The Romans did trade in Cornish tin, but not on a large scale.

Their invasion wasn't without resistance however, and in AD 60, Queen Boudica of the Iceni tribe from what is now East Anglia, led an uprising against the Romans. It started after the Queen's husband Prasutagus died, leaving his land to the Roman Emperor Nero, and his own two daughters. King Prasutagus had become a nominally independent ally of Rome, and taken loans to live a lavish lifestyle. On his death the Romans ignored his will, called in the loans, looted buildings, took slaves, flogged Boudica and raped her two young daughters - aged about 11 and 12.

After this outrage, Queen Boudica of the Iceni tribe, together with other tribes, said to number 30,000 men and women, massacred everyone in the Roman city of Colchester and 2,000 soldiers from the 9th legion who tried to stop them. They then marched on London and did the same, killing all who could not escape. Finally, Boudica was defeated by a Roman army led by Paulinus, the Governor of Britain, who had returned with his legion from Wales. Although greatly outnumbered, Paulinus commanded disciplined troops carrying two javelins each, shields and short stabbing swords. Boudica's troops were ill-equipped and trained, and funnelled into a crescent of inter-locking Roman shields, where they were brutally cut down. Few escaped the slaughter, including Boudica's fighting men and women and their families who came to watch. Not even their children or their livestock was spared. The exact location of the battle is not known, but thought to be somewhere on Watling Street. Boudica is said to have escaped, and died by her own hand by taking poison.

The main *perceived* threat to the Roman takeover of Britain wasn't so much Queen Boudica, but the Druids. The Druids were the priests of the early Celtic religion and operated on a class system. On the bottom rung were the serfs, then the warriors, with the Druid priests at the top. The priests were men of learning, and were the teachers, doctors, judges, poets and astrologers to the Celts. Training for an *apprenticeship in Druidism* could take up to twenty-years and was based on oral memorisation. Druids worshipped the sun and moon and took any celestial event as an omen, often requiring human sacrifice. They believed that the human soul didn't die, but after death passed from one person to another, in particular to a more prominent member of society. To the cultured Romans, the Druids were *noble savages*, revered for their mathematical and scientific knowledge, but feared for their barbarism. Often associated with Stonehenge in Wiltshire, their stronghold and spiritual home was the island of Anglesey off the coast of Wales, and that was where the Romans sent their legions to crush the Celts and their religious Druid leaders.

The Romans went prepared, lining up their flame-throwing catapults which were capable of shooting iron blocks and rocks 2,000 feet, from the edge of the Menai Strait. In addition, they had legions of cavalry who could ride across on their horses, and infantry with flat-bottomed boats. On the far side of the bank were the Celt warrior tribesmen banging their shields with the flat of their swords, cheering, jeering, and throwing insults at the Romans. The Druids priests invoked '*dark forces*' on the invaders, while the women danced naked through the ranks of their menfolk waving torches of fire. Fear gripped the Romans as never before, and they shook with terror.

When the battle began, the Roman's fear turned into fury, and they fought with such ferocity that it was to become legendary throughout Britain. None were spared but a handful of prisoners taken as slaves. Men, women and children were slaughtered. Many Druids were thrown alive onto burning fires in their own sacred groves of oak trees. The massacre of the Celts and Druids on the island of Anglesey lives on in history, and effectively put an end to Druidism in Britain.

The invasion of Britain by the Romans impacted little on Cornwall. However, some in the *country* of Cornwall flourished by trading raw materials with Roman merchants. Some took on their more cultured ways, learnt Latin, built villas in the Roman style, and cultivated their fields in long strips with heavy ploughs using slaves or serfs. East Cornwall was mined for tin, lead and silver, and these were traded with Roman merchants who exported it back to Rome – but trade up to AD 250 was small. This was due to the more accessible surface tin ore (cassiterite) the Romans could export from Spain and Brittany.

By AD 350, the Roman empire was being torn apart at its centre by civil war, and on its fringes barbarian invaders. In Britain, the Saxons were already starting to raid the south-east, which required extra finance to fund an army to hold them back, in addition to the forty thousand men protecting the Scottish and Welsh borders.

Roman civilization was based on city life, and although the countryside prospered by supplying food, the towns proved too expensive to be sustainable.

Spain was being ravished by barbarians, cutting off Rome's main source of tin. Also, the easily mined surface tin was being worked out, so Cornish tin came back in demand. Furthermore, trading with the peaceful Cornish became mutually beneficial without the need for legions of men, with the Romans paying cash in the form of copper and silver coins for tin ingots. All the Roman coins found in Cornwall date from this period, AD 250 - AD 350, and coins from that period have been found in the river Lerryn.

Eventually, the Romans left Britain in AD 410, because the islands had lost their strategic importance and the legions stationed there could be put to better use shoring up the Gaul frontier and guarding Italy. Thus, ended four centuries of Roman rule.

Cornish tin mines

Chapter Three:

Saxon, Anglo-Saxon and Viking Period
Early Medieval (Dark Ages)
AD 410 to AD 1066

When the Romans left England for good in AD 410, there would have been mixed feelings in Lanreath and the rest of Cornwall. For some, selling tin to the Roman merchants had prevented them from trading overseas, where the prices would have been better. Also, the wealth, culture and learning of Latin didn't filter down to those who mined the tin. In general, there would have been quiet jubilation for better times.

This new freedom and hope for future prosperity was not to last, as the Cornish began to learn of the new Saxon invaders. The next two centuries were known as the *Dark Ages*, because the Saxons systematically destroyed anything Roman. The illiterate, heathen Saxons thrust rapidly across England, pillaging, burning, slaughtering and enslaving any Romanized Britons who failed to escape to the relative safety of the Welsh mountains, or the remote Devonian peninsula. As the Saxons drove their way further and further west, the fear grew that they would eventually cross the Tamar, and pose a direct threat to the Cornish mines. Cornwall at this time was still unconquered.

In about AD 500, the British leader Ambrosias Aurelianus defeated the Saxons at Badon Hill, thought to be in Wiltshire, and halted their relentless push west. There followed half a century during which the Saxons consolidated their conquest, and a number of petty kingdoms emerged, the chief of which was Wessex.

Under the Saxon King Ceawlin, Dorset was overrun, and in AD 577 they defeated and killed three British kings who opposed them at Dyrham, just north of Bath. This cut off the Cornish Celts from their Welsh Celt cousins. The Cornish were now on their own. The few Romanized Cornish, together with Romanized English fugitives, established themselves as defenders of Roman civilisation against the Saxon barbarians, and as defenders of Roman Christianity against the invading heathens. Until this time only a few Cornish were Christian, but now they found themselves as the inheritors of a Christian faith that they were previously scarcely aware of. Thus, the Romanized Cornish and Romanized English fugitives became fanatically Christian, and rapidly converted as many of the population of Cornwall as they could, in order to bring a common cause for the expected battles.

But, the Saxons didn't follow up their success at Dyrham, and a century was to elapse before they pushed further west.

Castle Dore

In about AD 500 there were a number of Cornish kings, in effect tribal leaders, one of whom was the semi-historical King Mark. King Mark occupied Castle Dore, just a little west of Fowey, which was originally a small fortified village of the second century BC, but abandoned during the Roman period. The king had his subjects build his palace within the ramparts of Castle Dore, and being aware of the danger of the advancing barbaric, heathen Saxons, would also have wanted to protect his kingdom, which may have run from the Looe estuary to the Fowey estuary. Although not proven, it is probable that it was King Mark who had his subjects build the seven-mile long earth and stone-faced embankment known as the Giant's Hedge, in what is generally agreed to be a defensive position against the Saxon invaders.

The Giant's Hedge goes from the Lerryn river, a tributary of the Fowey estuary, through Willake Wood, passes just north of the village of Lanreath, heads down to Muchlarnick through Pelynt parish, and onwards to the West Looe river estuary. One of the best places to view the hedge now is just north of Lanreath village. Sadly, mechanised farming, together with cattle and sheep has destroyed much of the Giant's Hedge.

In 1756 Joshua Howell, a Rector of St Marnarch's church, together with William Borlase, a Cornish parson, geologist and historian,

24

rode the full length of the Giant's Hedge on horseback. Legend has it that *"Jack the Giant had nothing to do, so built a hedge from Lerryn to Looe."* As Jack, or *Cousin Jack* is synonymous with every Cornishman, the legend is not far from the truth! There are alternative versions of the rhyme, some with two giants and others saying the devil built it.

As Lanreath is located roughly halfway between Lerryn and Looe, and the Giant's Hedge skirts the village to the north and

Giant's Hedge on the edge of Lanreath village

east, the village folk of Lanreath were no doubt involved with the building. Indeed, as newly converted Christians, by necessity rather than conviction, it would have been their urgent duty to defend their kingdom from the Saxons, as tales of the barbaric acts of the invaders filtered through from those fleeing the occupied areas.

The son of a Romano-British priest called Patrick, converted Ireland to Christianity in the years from AD 431. The popular version is that Patrick was abducted as a 16 year old from western Britain early in the 5th Century, but escaped a number of years later. St Patrick, as he is now known, then returned to Ireland and successfully converted the Irish Pagan Druids to Christianity. The Druids of Ireland, like those of the Druids massacred at Anglesey by the Romans, were the upper-class of Irish society, philosophers, judges, teachers, historians, poets, musicians, physicians, astronomers and political advisors.

The truth however, partly in Patrick's own words in his *Confessio* tell a different story. Patrick's father was an aristocratic Decurion, an official employed by the Romans and responsible for collecting taxes. If he rid himself of this post to become a cleric as he wanted, his responsibilities would have fallen to his son Patrick. So, to escape this inherited poisoned chalice position in Roman Britain, Patrick fled to Ireland, taking with him his father's slaves to be sold to or traded with, wealthy Irish noblemen. This gained him an important social status and influence at the highest level. During his six-years in Ireland, Patrick developed a strong Christian faith and, on returning to England after the Romans departed, became a Bishop. He later returned to Ireland as a missionary. Patrick was so successful, no doubt using

St Patrick

his former wealthy friends to whom he sold slaves, that before long the Irish had their own missionaries eager to support the British against the invading heathen Saxons. It's doubtful Patrick *fully* converted anyone to Christianity, but rather added another God to the many pagan Gods of the Druids, and took ownership for Christianity. Some Druid pagan beliefs were brought to Cornwall by the early saints, such as holy wells and that mistletoe was the soul of an oak tree.

Most of the Irish missionaries were the sons and daughters of Celtic noblemen, who would have been schooled by the intellectual Druids in many things, including the arts. Their class structure and missionary zeal to convert the Cornish, and others, was no doubt with a gospel in one hand and a sword in the other. The Welsh also arrived as missionaries, including King Brychan, who came with his three wives, concubines, twenty four sons and twenty five daughters – all of them saints.

Unfortunately, most of the lives of the saints that were recorded and preserved in monasteries were destroyed during the Reformation, leaving only fables for future generations. However, we do know that a certain King Theodoric slew as many saints as he could catch, but as the title of *Saint* was bestowed without canonisation, we can only but wonder as to their number. In the sixth and seventh centuries, wave after wave of Irish saints, both men and women, landed on the shores of Wales, Cornwall and Brittany. Their names live on throughout Cornwall in particular, which has more villages and towns named after saints than anywhere in the world.

From about AD 500, a Christian building, or area, would have been in place in Lanreath. Maybe this was a stone, mud and wattle hut, with a cross as a point of worship. This would have stood on the ground on which St Marnarch's church now stands, and where the villagers would meet. Because Cornwall was never colonised by the Romans like the rest of Britain, but allowed to trade in tin under their overarching rule, Christian worship and practices must have been *unconventional*. Indeed, many saints were formally Druids, as were the Cornish Celts. *Romanized* Christianity had hardly touched Cornwall.

St Nun's, or St Ninnie's well,
in Pelynt parish

St Piran, the most famous Irish Saint, and reputed to be the first to land in Cornwall, was according to legend thrown off a cliff in Ireland during a storm tied to a millstone, but the sea calmed and he floated to Perranporth on the north Cornish coast.

St Piran - Truro Cathedral

One can imagine that the small community that lived within the ramparts of Bury Down, would have moved two miles south to settle within the relative safety of the Giant's Hedge, and under the protection of King Mark, or his descendents.

Just below the ridge on the edge of the village, on the southern slope, was a spring, then fertile ground leading down into the valley below.

There is a field in Lanreath known as *Burial Park*, which has never been archeologically surveyed. Could it be that this field was the burial grounds of the first Christians in Lanreath?

There is a second field in Lanreath known as *Sanctuary* – could this be the location of the place of worship in Lanreath? Or, maybe, where the village monk lived?

The prefix '*Lan*' stands for Christian Church, or monastic settlement, surrounded by a circular bank, and '*reath*', going back to the original name of Lanredock, suggests that Saint Rhydock, a holy man from Wales, may have had some connection with the village.

St Marnarch's, as the church ended up being called, was by all accounts an Irish monk. From what is known, Lanreath had a Christian community somewhere between AD 500 to AD 600, and a church in the form of a stone or wattle building with a thatched roof, where the monk may also have lived, on the site of the present church.

Established by, and revered by the saints were *holy wells*, that became a place of pilgrimage throughout Cornwall. Young girls would drop in pins, in the belief that the holy waters would tell them their wedding day, and folk would take water for its reputed healing properties. Belief in holy wells was a Druid tradition, and taken over by the early Christian saints, many of whom were schooled by Druids.

The well at Well Cottage - Lanreath

Lanreath has no record of a holy well, but the monastic settlement was established close to a spring that until the mid 20th century, was the main source of drinking water for the village.

If Lanreath did have a holy well, then the one built into the wall of what is now called Well Cottage, would be the obvious location. Even in drought years, this well still runs full, as if Saint Rhydock and Saint Marnarch were still looking after the village they Christianised.

By AD 530, most of England was Saxon and the people became known as Anglo-Saxons. Cornwall however, remained stubbornly Celtic, with its own king residing at Tintagel.

By AD 700, the Brythonic-speaking King Gerent was urged to adopt the practices of the Roman church by getting his clergy to cut their hair in a *halo* style, and calculate the date of Easter. The date was important so that the *Resurrection of the Saviour* fell on a *Sunday*, and didn't coincide with the Jewish holy day, the fourteenth of Nisan determined by the cycle of the moon. Both changes to practice were rejected by King Gerent. By AD 1100, or earlier, there was a church every three-miles throughout Cornwall, with the exception of the Moors. Cornwall was by now firmly, and fanatically, Roman Catholic.

The residents of Lanreath, together with other Cornish Celts, managed to fight off the Anglo-Saxons until the 8th or 9th Century, while at the same time carrying on farming the area.

If King Arthur existed, he may well have been Cornish and born at Tintagel castle, and if not a king, certainly a strong leader who would have fought the Saxon invaders. As legend has it, Dozmary Pool on Bodmin Moor, not far from Lanreath, was where King Arthur claimed the great sword *Excalibur,* and where it was thrown following his death.

Dozmary Pool - where 'Excalibur' was thrown after Arthur's death

By this time, Cornwall was known as *Kernow*, and the Celts continued to speak their own language. Many Cornish names have their origins from this early medieval period. Lanreath parish is unusual to have a higher proportion of non-Cornish names in the area. This gives credence to the speculation that the Saxons resided in Lanreath, and may have lived on the north ridge of the village.

'*Bod*' was dwelling, as in Bodmin. '*Lan*' (ancient church) as in Lanreath, or Landrake would date from this time, or maybe earlier, with the Welsh Celts using the double '*L*', as in Llanelli.

It's reasonable to suppose that here in this Lanreath valley, perhaps on the very spot where the parish church now stands, there dwelt a small community of Celtic monks, or at least a single monk.

King Mark, often associated with the Arthurian stories, is said to have ruled the area around Lanreath and a few miles away. On the other side of the Fowey River, an ancient memorial stone commemorates the existence of Mark's nephew, the even more celebrated Tristan. The fable goes: Tristan journeyed to Ireland to be cured by the skilled Isolde of a battle wound. On hearing of her beauty and skills, King Mark sent his nephew Tristan back to Ireland to woo her for him and bring her back to Cornwall to be his betrothed. Isolde's mother gave a handmaiden a *love potion*, with strict instructions to give it to Isolde on her wedding night. However, Tristan and Isolde accidentally drank it on their journey back to Cornwall, and they fell deeply in love. Although King Mark married Isolde, her love affair with Tristan continued, and

when King Mark found out, he forgave her but banned Tristan from Cornwall. At first Tristan moved to King Arthur's court, then to Brittany where he married Iseult, but didn't consummate the marriage because of his love for Isolde. After falling ill with another battle wound, he sent for Isolde in the hope that she would cure him. If she agreed, the sails of the boat would be white, or if not, the sails would be black. Tristan's wife Iseult on seeing the white sails told him they were black, and Tristan died of grief. Soon after, Isolde died of a broken heart

Tristan stone at Fowey – such was her love for him.

Around AD 710 the Saxons eventually invaded Cornwall after the death of King Arthur. Several battles took place over the next 50 years, with the Saxons mainly victorious. In AD 807 the Viking Danes formed an alliance with the Cornish against the Saxons. Seven years later, the Saxon, Egbert of Wessex, conquered Cornwall, but was unsuccessful in subjugating the people. These battles were raids by the English into a foreign territory. The rewards for the conqueror were of course land, which the English king gave his nobles in exchange for military and political support.

Some Cornish who lost their lands during this time fled to Brittany, which became known as *Little Britain*, thus the name *Great Britain* was used for the British Isles. Some of those, who were now called *Bretons*, returned with William the Conqueror hoping to get back their ancestral forbearers' lands.

Few Saxons ever actually settled in Cornwall, but collections of Saxon coins, jewellery, gold and silver have been found. Tresawson Farm, close to Lanreath, is reputed to be the last Saxon farm established in their push into Cornwall. Many believe that the Saxons resided in Lanreath, in particular along a ridge to the north of the village. Old maps show one field to have been an ancient burial park. As this ridge-line is just above the huge defensive earth embankment known as the Giant's Hedge, and as the area is festooned with springs and streams, this would have made a perfect location for the Saxons to settle.

Tresawson Farm - reputed to be the last Saxon farm in Cornwall

The Cornish Celts, sometimes with their allies the Vikings, fought the Anglo-Saxons for hundreds of years. The last Cornish King, Doniert, drowned in the Golitha Falls in AD 875 on the River Fowey near St Cleer, not far from Lanreath. However, it was not until AD 926, saddened and weary, that the Cornish Celts were finally beaten. The victor, Saxon King Athelstan, became the overlord in Cornwall, setting the border with England at the River Tamar. As all Cornish people that were living beyond the new border were sent back, Lanreath must have seen an influx to its population.

Although the Vikings had once been Cornwall's ally against the Saxons, who were terrorising the English and plundering their villages and churches, in AD 981 the Vikings turned against the Celts and invaded what is now Padstow. They destroyed most of the town, including St Petroc's church. The Cornish now had a new enemy.

King Doniert's stone

By the year 1050, more than two centuries after Egbert's conquest, the Saxon subjugation of Cornwall must have been fairly complete, stronger in the east, then rapidly declining beyond the line of the Camel and Fowey rivers, leaving Lanreath just within as the last area of Saxon influence.

Golitha Falls where King Doniert died

33

Battle of Hastings from the Bayeux tapestry

Chapter Four:

Norman Period - Medieval Times - AD 1066 to AD 1485

As most people know, in 1066, William of Normandy, better known as William the Conqueror, defeated the English King Harold at the Battle of Hastings, and named himself king of England. What is less well known is that he defeated the English with the help of 6,000 Bretons, a third of his army, including many Cornish, whose ancestors had fled Cornwall during the Saxon invasion. Without them, William's invasion of England might have failed. The Celtic Bretons were fearsome spear-throwing mounted cavalry, and archers noted for their tactics of aiming their arrows into the sky to rain down on their enemy. It may well be that it was a Breton of Cornish descent, who shot the fatal arrow that pierced the eye of King Harold, and thus changed the course of British history.

By 1072 England was completely subjugated, and William turned his attention to the consolidation of his conquest. This he achieved by a systematic extension of the feudal system, whereby all land belonged to the king, who passed it on to those he favoured, in return for supplying men for military service. Thus, landless serfs in Cornwall became reliant for their existence on their feudal *Lord of the Manor*. Land was also sub-leased by the Lord under tenancy agreements to gain income. Wealth therefore depended on land holdings.

Most people in England, and certainly the Celts of Cornwall, considered the land beyond the Tamar as a separate country. Indeed, Cornwall had its own language, weights and measures, and its own laws. English landowners had been gradually taking over Cornish land, and with a new king in England, even more land was being taken.

King William gave most Cornish land to his friends and family. What infuriated the Cornish most was that he made his half-brother, Robert of Mortain, the Earl of Cornwall, and invested him with two-thirds of the manors in Cornwall, as well as land in England. In total, eight-hundred manors in twenty counties were seized, plus land owned by the church, including the manors of St Petroc in Bodmin and the Bishop of Exeter's manor of St Germans. It's recorded that the Abbot of Tavistock complained that Robert of Mortain had seized four manors that had been purchased by the church. These Christian Normans, descendants of the Vikings and successors to the Saxons, were brutal in business at the expense of the Cornish gentry and peasants alike. Cornish men, no doubt including men living in Lanreath, were forcibly stopped from mining minerals, tending animals and growing food for

Restormel Castle

their families, and put to work building defensive castles at Launceston, Trematon and Restormel, and churches like St Marnarch's in Lanreath. So, the next time you walk around and admire your Norman church, spare a thought for the Cornish serfs and slaves who contributed their labour with blood, sweat and tears, and many with their lives, so that the faithful would have somewhere they could worship.

In 1086 William ordered a countrywide land census known now as the Doomsday Book because it was so comprehensive and final. Like the *Day of Judgment,* as it has been called, there was no appeal to the taxes set by the doomsday assessors. Lanreath parish is recorded as covering an area of a hundred and forty acres. There were forty acres of woodland, thirty acres of pasture supporting three head of cattle, sixty sheep, and enough arable land to provide work for eight ploughs, although there were only three ploughs in the village. It's likely that these ploughs were shared between fifteen or so resident families. As these statistics related only to land and possessions that could be taxed, the true figures would have been many times those recorded.

Yet the Normans were not numerous, probably no more than eighty lords of manors, many with Cornish estates, but living elsewhere in England. Their power however was out of all proportion to their numbers. Supporting King William were Bretons of Cornish descent, who fought with him at the Battle of Hastings against the Anglo-Saxon King Harold, and for their reward were given minor manors, or their family's ancestral lands back.

These Cornish Bretons would have spoken Brythonic (Cornish Celtic), almost indistinguishable from the Breton Celtic language, their Norman masters French, the Cornish upper-class emigrants and east Cornish, English, and the clergy, Latin, albeit badly in an effort to cling onto their Roman Catholic roots, which they did for the next 350 years.

For the businesslike Normans the English clergy at that time would have been a push-over, being married, easy-going, inefficient, and in appearance scarcely distinguishable from their parishioners. Their monasteries and churches were small hovels, and reliant on some foreign house outside of Cornwall for finance. Many were therefore replaced by Noman clergymen with a higher religious status, and acting as *spiritual drill sergeants*.

In the 20 years between the Conquest and Doomsday, the Count of Mortain exploited Cornwall financially and disrupted economic life by asset-stripping the vast number of manors he acquired. The Doomsday Book records for instance, that Tucowit manor was worth 5 shillings, whereas when acquired it was worth 60 shillings. Tolgollow Manor was worth 4 shillings, whereas when acquired it was worth 20 shillings, and Trecow and Gear manors each declined from 25 shillings to 5 shillings. This exploitation of Cornish land by the first Earl of Cornwall drained the economy and started an economic decline. Cornwall is still, centuries later, an economically poor county compared to the rest of the United Kingdom, and still has vast tracts of land in the hands of royalty.

As structure took place, with it came the introduction of the tithe system. It is not known exactly when the *original* Tithe Barn in Lanreath was built, but a secure barn would have been

Current Tithe Barn and Tithe Cottage   needed about 1090-1095

37

as a collecting centre for tithes. Tithes were taxes on people collected by and for the benefit of the clergy. Clergy were normally appointed by the Lord of the Manor as their sponsor. As the manorial lord was responsible for the appointment, most of the time it was kept within the family – the calling to amass wealth being stronger than a calling to minister to the poor. Essentially, people had to pay a tenth of their annual income to the clergy. Payment was *in kind*, so the tenth chicken, tenth cow or tenth measure of corn. The clergy used what they needed and stored the balance in a tithe barn, or sold it on.

Tithes in AD 786 were arbitrary and could be paid to the clergy of choice, but with the establishment of parishes in England, tithes went to the parish priest, or rector. In 1836 the Tithe Commutation Act came into force, that changed payment in kind to payment in cash, and detailed tithe maps and field size records produced. Records for the 17th March, 1842, show that Lanreath parish had not less than two-thirds of land subject to tithe payments, with the Reverend Richard Buller being the recipient of all tithes. This amounted to 4,300 acres, bringing in a total of £522.1s.0d.

The lords of the manors owned the right to mill grain from all of their estates, bringing in a valuable source of revenue. In Lanreath the original grain processing unit was located at Bogga Mill, where there was a reliable supply of water.

Typical hand-operated quern

A later mill thought to be 19th century was located in what is now a paddock just beyond the Cob Cottages, and although the water wheel has long since rotted away, the pit structure still remains, as does a shaft going into a nearby building. Water was stored in a control-pond above the wheel, and let out during the hours of milling. Anyone found milling their own grain using a *quern* by the lord's bailiff would have been heavily fined.

Medieval criminals when caught would be locked in wooden stocks, and the local people encouraged to throw rotten food at them – this certainly happened in Lanreath, and the stocks can still be seen in the porch of St Marnarch's church. One thing of interest is that the stocks have seven holes, the last hole reputed to be for a one-legged rogue who lived in the village at the time they were made.

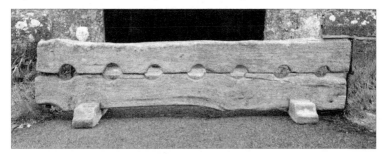

The seven-holed stocks outside St Marnarch's church

The Saxons were heathens who destroyed anything established by Roman Christianity, and although converted to Christianity later, would not have added value to any building that the monks and early Lanreath Christians built. It can be assumed therefore, that nothing much existed before the Normans commenced the present building sometime after 1066, starting with the Nave and Transept walls. The exact date of the building of the original Norman church is unknown, but a *minor* church is *assumed* to have existed at Doomsday, as the village is recorded as *Lan*redock - church site. Whether this was the original mud and wattle building established by the Druid-Christian monks, or something more substantial, is not recorded. A blocked off entrance to the Norman church can be seen on the north side, but this may have been built later to '*let the devil out during christenings.*'

Blocked up north door

Inside, part of the original

39

Norman altar stone, measuring 18" long, 13" wide, and 7" high, can be found on the windowsill of the Lady Chapel. The font standing at the rear of the church was also Norman, although the beautifully carved font cover was Jacobean.

Original Norman altar stone

The size of the church was a testimony to the importance of Lanreath to the Normans, sited as it was with an abundance of spring water and streams, a high earthen security wall running between two estuaries, and a nearby ready-made fortification giving views up to 20 miles in all directions.

Norman font

By 1201 King John was on the throne. At this time, Cornish miners were angry because of the high taxes that were placed on tin, and mining restrictions. To placate the population, King John brought back the old Stannary laws that allowed tinners freedom from ordinary laws and gave them *special rights*. These included the rights to dig for tin wherever they wanted, and lay claim by bounding the area with turf. A tin bound generally consisted of about an acre of land that had four corners. Each corner was required to have six turfs, or stones, with a total of 24 for each bound. Tinners were allowed to divert and use water for streaming that separated tin from other minerals. As trees were in short supply, estates banned them from being used to make charcoal for smelting in blowing houses. The *right of turbary*, therefore, allowed peat cutting on the moors, with the turfs being turned into charcoal. Peat charcoal is said to give a finer grained better quality tin. They were also allowed to appoint their own warden to make sure that the miners were treated fairly, although they still had to pay taxes, *toll tin*, to the king.

Thus, the tin industry had its own laws, privileges, and Stannary Courts administered from a variety of buildings and locations in the coinage towns at Liskeard, Lostwithiel, Truro and Helston. In Lostwithiel was the *Great Court*, where the Sheriff and Stannators met. Then, the *Coinage* or *Assay Hall*, where the quality of tin was assessed. Next, the *Weighing Hall*, before duty was calculated by the *Exchequer* or *Banking House*, with the ingots being stored in a vaulted cellar below known as the *Tynne Porch*, for safekeeping until sale and shipment. In 1644 the Great Hall was burnt out, following which the Stannary parliament used the Exchequer building for meetings - now mistakenly referred to as the Duchy Palace.

The term *coinage* comes from the old French word *coin*, meaning a corner, and referred to a small piece of tin cut from the corner of the block by the assay master to determine the quality.

There developed, inevitably, a strong tradition of smuggling untaxed tin abroad. This started with wandering *tinkers* who purchased un-coined ore by the pound from the stream works and blowing houses, then converted it into *pocket tin*. These small tin blocks would then be sold to seamen and travelling pewterers, or smuggled by night aboard ships that docked at Fowey and Mevagissey, ostensibly to buy Cornish slate and stone.

The law for wrong-doers was harsh however, with a jail adjoining the Stannary building. Prisoners were often hanged first then tried afterwards, with those found *not* guilty being allowed a priest to pray for their souls.

In 1215 King John put his seal on a document called the Magna Carta, giving certain rights to ordinary people. The Magna Carta confirmed that Cornwall was a separate nation

Hanging at Bodmin jail

from England with its own government, as medieval maps show. The most famous being the Mappa Mundi, drawn by monks in 1290 and on display in Hereford Cathedral.

King Edward III re-confirmed in 1328 that Cornwall was a separate country from England, and ruled that it was to be owned by his son and not him. This resulted in the setting up of the Duchy of Cornwall in 1337, which exists until this day. One surviving rule is that the possessions of any person dying in Cornwall without a Will, son or descendents, is taken by the Duchy – currently Prince Charles. Thus, for instance, Restormel Castle, lands in Lostwithiel, and parts of the Fowey river estuary currently used for commercial shell fishing by the Duchy, was acquired for free by the Crown on the death of Edmond in 1299, the last Earl of Cornwall, who died without a son or heir.

The Punch Bowl Inn was probably built about the time the Normans built the Lanreath church. Indeed, it could well have been a church house with multi-functional uses, including the brewing of ale for church celebrations. The current cellar was thought to be a blacksmith's shop, opening out onto the street, and the kitchen the original court house. This speculation is consistent with the Normans imposing law and order through their own clergy, and displaying power with impressive buildings. It would be a few centuries later before the court moved to the manor house we know as Court Barton, and the building became an inn in 1620.

Lanreath has seen many changes, and faced many challenges, but none more devastating than the *Black Death* (bubonic plague), which came in phases over a three hundred year period. Fear gripped the village which went into lockdown, in particular for three years from 1348, although the plague didn't reach Cornwall until the winter of 1349. The people of Lanreath would have thought the plague was a punishment from God, so special prayers needed to have been said in St Marnarch's church, imploring him to forgive their sins. Some carried charms, some sniffed sweet smelling herbs and spices, and others tried eating cooked frogs and mice to ward off the unseen death. Those afflicted developed a rash, which then turned into disgusting black boils, sometimes the size of apples, that when burst oozed out a foul-smelling pus. Death would follow in a matter of hours, or a few days. Rectors of churches were not spared. In a ten-year period up to 1349, the Bishop of Exeter approved the appointment of an average of four rectors per year in Cornwall. From the late winter of 1349 until the winter of 1350, 85 were appointed. John de Restrawel, the Rector of Lanreath between 1333-1358, survived.

In 1610, Court Barton was built facing north towards the church, with no windows south to maximize the sun and stunning views. This could in part reflect the fear and superstition of the day that the plague

42

was brought by the wind or the devil, both of which were assumed to originate from the south. The Pilgrim Fathers leaving England in 1620, also built their houses in America without south-facing windows. When

Court Barton - south-facing wall

the plague came to Cornwall, no one would have been allowed in or out of villages such as Lanreath, People were dying at an alarming rate, not knowing from where it came and when it would end. When it finally left, the Cornish population had been devastated, leaving no family or village untouched.

The long-held belief is that the cause of the Black Death was fleas that picked up bacteria from infected rats, which bit and infected people. The infected rats came from China carried on ships. In 1349 the plague killed half of Truro, and in 1350, 1,500 people died in Bodmin. The Duke of Buckingham's army billeted in Plymouth lost a quarter of its men. Although not recorded, a third of the population of Lanreath could have died from the plague, as in the rest of Cornwall, and half the population of England.

In the aftermath, some corrupt landlords took advantage by taking over common land that had been used by villagers, and filled it with sheep, thus depriving those remaining of access to grazing land, hay for their remaining animals, and firewood for cooking.

The sudden shortage of labour had dramatic social and economic effects on the population of Cornwall, insofar as the lords of the manors were faced with labourers demanding higher wages. This in turn led to the rise in prices, and the start of a breakdown of the former feudal system.

The peasants were also becoming disenchanted with an unfair poll tax levied by an incompetent government, and the corruption of the clergy, as well as the church hierarchy. Led by Wycliffe, open-air preaching by poor priests called Lollards gained popularity, especially as they were preaching against the wealth of the church and the clergy.

Many of the clergy had no special calling and supplemented their income in all sorts of ways, including illegal trafficking and renting out church property. Some of the canons at the collegiate church at Crantock, for example, let out their houses to laymen, for uses including taverns and

Crantock church

brothels. At Glasney College, a large amount of church property went missing, including ornaments, vestments and money. When the *Peasant's Revolt,* as it was called, reached Cornwall, the officiating priest and clergy were assaulted in Crantock Church. John Calesteke, the priest in charge, was dragged through the streets of Penryn and bound to a cross. In St Hilary parish, John Browder was seized and bound, and another priest, Walter Sabcre, then cut off his head which was carried to London on a spear. Today, over 650 years later, when the church sells glebe land for building, special conditions apply to prevent this happening again. That is, no alcohol can be sold, and houses can't be used for immoral purposes. All the houses on the east side of Lanreath that were built on former church land, have covenants on them with these restrictions.

The Peasant's Revolt, fuelled by the speeches and rhymes of John Ball, was more widespread in England than Cornwall. It was a Cornishman called Robert Tresilian, however, who was appointed Lord Chief Justice, and hanged many serfs for no more than rising up to ask for liberty. Many others were hung, drawn and quartered, others disembowelled. John Ball was captured and given a barbarous death. In the end, Robert Tresilian himself was denounced as a traitor and hanged at Tyburn, and had some of his estates confiscated. Sir John Colshull married his widow, and gained the manor of Tremodret in Duloe, just three-miles from Lanreath, where the chancel aisle of the church houses the tombs and effigies of his family.

Tomb of Sir John Colshull - Duloe Church

Shortly after this at the Battle of Agincourt, King Henry V achieved his victory over the French, and a generation or so later rival Plantagenets plunged into a struggle, still known as the War of the Roses.

The 15th century brought more new buildings with fresh trends in architecture, and like many other churches St Marnarch's was once again enlarged, acquiring a tall and splendid tower. With this, the Middle Ages came to an end.

The 'so called' Bishop's chair
St Marnarch's church, Lanreath

This chair, as far as is known, was one of three that was made for the Grylls family of Lanreath in about 1610, on the completion of Court Barton. The chair is Jacobean in style. When the family left the village, they donated the chairs to St Marnarch's church. The whereabouts of one is unknown, but may not have been donated to the church, and one was sold by the church at auction, leaving just one. A local carpenter in Looe kindly made a cradle for free, so that when the Bishop of Truro visited Lanreath on the 25th November 2012, he would be able to sit on it without any danger - to him or the chair.

Bishop Tim of Truro at St Monarch's church on 25th November 2012

Chapter Five:

Tudor Period - AD 1485 – AD 1603

In 1485 an important battle took place known as the *Battle of Bosworth Field* that ended the War of the Roses. During this battle the last Plantegenet king, Richard III was killed. Henry Tudor had led the winning side and seized the crown to become King Henry VII, the first of the Tudor dynasty.

Boconnoc estate

The new king had Celtic ancestors from Wales, so that made him popular with the Cornish. Cornish people, including villagers from Lanreath, had fought for Henry at the Battle of Bosworth Field after being led to believe that he was a descendant of King Arthur. With the battle won, the new king gave Boconnoc Estate, just four miles from Lanreath to Edward Curtenay, and made him the new Earl of Devon.

Henry angered the Cornish people by appointing his three-year old son, Prince Arthur, Duke of Cornwall, and gave him the mines of Herodsfoot and Botelet, as well as the tin mines in Cornwall becoming part of the Duke's land. He then imposed extra taxes on the Cornish to pay for a war in Scotland. The final straw came when the Duchy abolished the Stannary Laws that had given Cornish miners special rights for nearly 300 years.

Cornishmen were extremely angry, so in 1497, an army of about 15,000 Cornish led by a Bodmin lawyer, Thomas Flamank, and blacksmith Michael Joseph, but known as *An Gof*, marched towards London. The plan was to meet with the king and ask him to restore the Stannary Laws. In case they met the king's army first, they armed themselves with locally-made farming tools such as pitchforks, scythes and hammers.

Nearing London, they met King Henry's 10,000-strong army, and were quickly beaten back. Some were taken prisoner, others escaped, but An Gof and Thomas Flamank were captured and brutally put to death. Some unlucky Cornish prisoners were sold as slaves, their

Thomas Flamank and An Gof

property and land taken, but many were spared. After the rebellion, life went back to normal. People mined, farmed, and those from Lanreath attended St Marnarch's church and the Catholic masses once again. Later, King Henry restored the Stannary Laws and gave even more rights to the Cornish miners.

In memory of the Cornish Rebellion, the children of St Keverne unveiled a statue in 1997.

Lanreath was, as most of Cornwall, fearfully independent and related more to Wales and Brittany through its Celtic language roots than Saxon / Norman England. Cornish was widely spoken. Priests at Mass went on reading from the Catholic Prayer Book in Latin. This prevented the people from understanding the Bible for themselves, and preserved the mystique of the Roman Catholic church. English was a foreign language as far as most Cornish people were concerned.

Services were held behind *rood screens* that cut-off the people from the clergy, so they could only glimpse at what was going on. On the top of the rood screen was a *rood beam*, that gave support to a *gallery,* or *loft*. The *rood* is the cross (rod/pole) with the figure of Christ, usually flanked by the Virgin Mary and St John. These galleries had various uses, including a place for a choir for singing and for the reading of the gospel. The original doors and stairs to the rood galleries still remain in many churches, but the high galleries were in the main all destroyed.

Rood screen at St Marnarch's church - minus beam, loft or gallery

Opening to rood gallery or loft   *Space for rood beam and access*

Henry VIII became king in 1509 and had a girl child with Catherine of Aragon, but no male heir. Thus, he decided to divorce and marry Anne Boleyn. The Pope, however, refused permission, so in 1534 Henry declared himself head of a new Church of England and married Anne anyway, causing the Pope to excommunicate him from the Roman Catholic church. Again, there was a lot of anger in Cornwall, as the people had been Roman Catholic since the time of the saints.

Across Cornwall, as in England, Henry ordered monasteries to be closed and assets taken. After Henry died in 1547 and Edward VI became king, the government sent officers around Cornwall to remove and destroy any former Catholic objects of worship, extending to churches and objects of veneration. Although this didn't include rood lofts, or galleries, many were destroyed anyway.

In 1549 parliament passed the *Act of Uniformity*, by legalizing Archbishop Cranmer's original prayer book in English. This was to be used in church services, replacing the old one that was written in Latin. The Cornish speaking population generally didn't read, speak or understand English, but were well used to hearing Latin in their services and wanted it to stay that way. For a time parliament allowed the Cornish language to be used in their church services, and Latin to read the Bible. Then all this changed and they insisted they read the new prayer book in English, not a word of which most spoke, or wanted to speak.

With the harsh winds of change forcing the introduction of the English Prayer Book, rebellion was in the air. Bishop Veysay at Exeter was preaching the new order. The king was to be acknowledged as the supreme head of the church, all popish idolatry was to be abolished, relics were to be taken away and the Bible was to be set up in churches.

Archbishop Cranmer

Also, the Paternoster (Lord's Prayer), Creed (statement of faith) and the Ten Commandments were to be taught and read in English. There were to be no more pilgrimages, no more superstitious observations of holy days, and births, deaths and marriages were to be registered.

Cornwall was in uproar, and support was given to them by the men from Devon. The Cornish people followed their Catholic priests and leaders by rebelling. One of the leaders of the *Prayer Book Rebellion* was John Winslade of Tregarrick in Pelynt Parish, a large landowner, rebel, and defender of the Catholic faith. Under the leadership of Henry Bray the Mayor of Bodmin, and Sir Humphrey Arundell, they formed an army and marched into battle. The Protestant English killed them in great numbers on the battleground, and thousands died fighting. Their final stand was in West Devon at Sampford Courtnay, where 5,500 Cornishmen were killed, farmers, miners and tradesmen, some fighting with little more than pitchforks. Eventually, the king's army killed the Cornish priests and leaders by hanging them, then dismembering their bodies as a warning. After one battle, the English took 900 Cornish prisoners, tied them up and cut their throats. Lanreath, just two-miles from Pelynt, would not have been left untouched.

The king's soldiers arrived in Pelynt looking for John Winslade, marching past the church and on to the estate of Tregarrick. This was the first and only military action ever to take place in the village, but he wasn't at home. He was finally captured in Bodmin, taken to London to be tried, then hung, drawn and quartered at Tyburn on 27th January 1550. All his land was given away, except Tregarrick that he had passed to his wife Agnes, and on her death, to his son William. However, Agnes married again to John Trevanion, who sold it to the Bullers, Mohuns and Trelawnys behind her back, to make sure that William Winslade never inherited his father's estate on the death of his mother.

So in the end the Cornish Prayer Book Rebellion was brutally subdued, and the English language gradually became the language of Cornwall, setting in place the biggest casualty, the decline of the Cornish language forever.

Before this finally happened however, a number of what were called *Miracle Plays* were written in Cornish. These were satirical and openly performed, poking fun at the English without them knowing it. Some are still performed today by groups of Cornish actors, and still in the Cornish language.

Tregarrick - John Winslade's former home

The destruction stopped during the reign of Catholic Queen Mary, *Bloody Mary*, but restarted with a vengeance on her death in 1558, to include all painted images, pictures and assumed faces of worship in stain glass windows. Destruction stopped again in 1560. It was Elizabeth I, *The Virgin Queen*, who ordered the Tables of Commandments to be hung-up in the east end of the chancel in churches. They can still be seen in St Marnarch's church today. The *Word*, Elizabeth decreed, being more powerful than *idols*. Fortunately, the original order to destroy the figures of adoration on the rood screens that separated the clergy from the people, didn't include the panels below. Some of the rood screens with painted images therefore survived the extreme destruction by puritanical zealots during the reigns of Edward VI and Elizabeth I, but most in St Marnarch's church didn't. Some of the painted screens in the church that weren't completely scrubbed out, were restored later to an unusual high quality. Today, they are said to be the best-painted rood screen panels in Cornwall, looking like Flemish paintings with landscape backdrops, rather than the usual stock figures.

1   2   3   4   5

(1) As in some other paintings found in Cornish churches, this one of Jesus holding an orb, has a beard but lacks a moustache
(2) A *monkish* King Henry VI with his white hart, a saint in waiting until King Henry VIII married Anne Boleyn and dashed his hopes
(3) This painting of the Virgin Mary is partially damaged, but clearly shows her carrying Jesus in her womb
(4) St Elizabeth, cousin of the Virgin Mary and mother of John the Baptist. Also visibly pregnant, it is likely that expectant mothers would have knelt at the spot to pray. Being close the Mary suggests a meeting as described in St Luke's Gospel
(5) St Ursula, could have been a Romano-British virgin and martyred with 11,000 maidens - seen holding an arrow that killed her

6   7   8   9

(6) Pope Gregory the Great who in AD 597 sent Augustine to convert Anglo-Saxon England

(7) St Jerome, a Roman Christian priest, theologian and historian

(8) St Ambrose, born into a Roman Christian family, he became Bishop of Milan and gave a lot of his money to the poor

(9) St Augustine of Hippo from Roman Africa, was a great thinker and theologian, he framed the concept of original sin and just war

10   11   12   13

(10) St Apollonia, patron of those with toothache, shown with her 'pincers' as she lost all her teeth

(11) St Sitha (Zita) the gentle housekeeper with her giant key

(12) St Dorothy, with a basket of three apples and three roses picked from the garden of Jesus as proof that there is a heaven

(13) St Barbara, the virgin saint who was imprisoned by her pagan father in a tower. She then angered her father by having a builder put three windows in a newly constructed bath house to represent the Holy Trinity. She was eventually beheaded by her own father

Court Barton - former manor home of the Grylls family

The famous hearth in the panelled room at Court Barton

Chapter Six:

Stuart Period - AD 1603 to AD 1714

At the end of the reign of the Tudors in 1603, and the start of the reign of the Stuarts when King James I of Scotland also became king of England, it was impossible to exaggerate the importance of the gentry in Cornwall. They were all landowners, magistrates, commanders of the land and sea forces, and parliamentary members for the county. At this time forty five Cornish manors were held by the Duchy, the tenants of whom were Cornish gentlemen, mostly related to each other directly or through marriage. The still common phrase *"Cousin Jack"*, refers to the closeness of the Cornish to each other through their former allegiances to their Lord of the Manor, and the inter-relationship of the gentry.

Notable among them were the Godolphins of Godolphin, Vyvyans of Trelowarren, Bassets of Tehidy, St Aubyns of Clowance, Killigrews of Arwennack, Trevanions of Caerhays, Arundells of Trerice, Arundells of Lanherne, Treffrys of Fowey, Trelawnys of Trelawne, Mohuns of Boconnoc, Eliots of Port Eliot, Carews of Antony, Bullers of Shillingham, Edgcumbes of Cotehele and Mount Edgcumbe, Grenvilles of Stowe, and the Grylls of Court Barton in Lanreath village and others whose inheritance and influence were scarcely less. The extreme Catholics had been weeded out, the Winslades of Pelynt next to Lanreath Parish and the Treians were gone, and the Lanherne Arundells reduced.

In the late 16th century, branches of the Grylls family had moved to Lanreath. The family had established itself with William Grylls who was born at Liskeard, went to Oxford and gained a law degree, then ended up in Tavistock. There he became a man of influence running town affairs, owning a law practice, and being a tin merchant. In 1577 he purchased a coat-of-arms that his descendents have used ever since. The eldest son of William Grylls was Charles, also an attorney, and it was Charles who purchased the land on which Court Barton now stands.

National Archives documents show Charles Grylls purchased Court from John Chudleigh of Ayrston in Devon a little before 1598, being a mortgagee of Hugh Trevanion. It is probable therefore, that he lived there for some years before re-building.

In 1610 Charles Grylls son, John, began building the Jacobean manor house called Court, now known as Court Barton, but it is unknown what was on the site before then. One has to assume that a house existed when it was purchased.

Charles died in 1611, and in 1623 his son John (later Sir John), commissioned a glorious memorial to his father, his mother Agnes, and their eight children. This is still a major attraction in St Marnarch's church today. John completed building Court Barton in 1612. The completion date was originally over the granite doorway entrance, as recorded by a C.S. Gilbert in 1817, but has since disappeared.

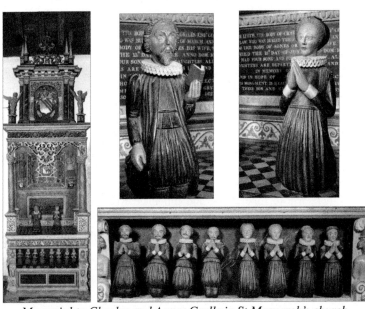

Memorial to Charles and Agnes Grylls in St Marnarch's church

The room to the left of the main entrance, in addition to being the main living space, was also *The Justice Hall*, where the manor court was held. On the way in, one would have passed a small room that was used as *The Armoury*, with the deliberate intention, no doubt, of showing guests and villains who was in charge.

At this time piracy was a major problem, with the Cornish being both perpetrators and victims. England was at peace with Spain after a twenty year war, but the Dutch were getting the better of the Spanish and captured Channel ports. Dunkirk was captured and used as the base for privateers who preyed on English shipping. One Dunkirker took four ships off The Lizard in a single day, two of them coming from Looe and two from Fowey. Even worse were Mohammedan pirates from Algiers and Salee in Morocco on the Barbary Coast, who concentrated on the western approaches hovering off Cornwall and Scilly. At this time, slavery was a very profitable business for those who specialized in this trade. During one ten day period in 1625 they took twenty seven ships and two hundred men, including eighty from Looe. A few weeks earlier, sixty men, women and children had been snatched out of a church on Mount's Bay, and carried off into slavery. In a single month in 1636, the Algerine and Salee pirates captured fifteen fishing boats from Looe and Helford. Castles such as Pendennis in Falmouth and St Mawes on the opposite bank, built in 1539, did their best to protect ships in the estuary, but nothing could protect ships in the English Channel. Firing cannon balls into the estuary was the way of warning everybody of a pending shipping violation, and many of these are still found by divers today.

Pendennis castle   *Inside Pendennis castle*

However, ships captured by the Cornish and brought into the estuary were a valuable source of income, and although illegal, the gentry and the inhabitants supported it and saw it as a *Gift from God*. Indeed, when a Spanish ship carrying silver had been wrecked off The Lizard, the local Lord of the Manor, Killigrew, led the local inhabitants in trying to salvage the treasure, and threatened death to anyone who interfered.

It is doubtful that anyone from Lanreath was involved in piracy, or was taken into slavery, as the Grylls family were well-established and curried favour with the king. Indeed, John Grylls was informed by the king that he was to be appointed High Sheriff of Cornwall in 1641. His brother Charles would have congratulated him on the news, as would the Reverend Francis Grylls the incumbent Rector of St Marnarch's church.

The current oak-panelled room at Court Barton has changed little since then, but during a 21 year period in the 18th century when the property was thrown into chancery, the mansion was greatly neglected. Many valuable pieces of carving, together with the armour from the Justice Hall, were taken away. Parts of the roof of the panelled room collapsed, and during restoration some of the family shields were partly covered up. The main focus of interest was the ornate fireplace with its three shields. John Grylls commissioned these at the time of his marriage to Grace Bere, incorporating the Grylls and Bere coats of arms into the design. The three shields above the fireplace are:

Grylls   *Grylls and Bere*   *Bere*

With a history of supporting English royalty, the Cornish gentry continued their allegiance when King Charles I, an arrogant and obstinate man, who became embroiled in serious arguments with parliament, dividing England into two sides. On one side were the supporters of parliament, nicknamed the *Roundheads*, and on the other were the *Royalists, or Cavaliers*, that supported King Charles I. The Grylls family and people of Lanreath, together with most of Cornwall, were Royalists. The Cornish once again, prepared themselves for war.

The years leading up to the Civil War were tough for Cornish fishermen, with pirates sighted daily off the coast. To add to this misery, many peasants and tinners were required for the war in Scotland, leaving too few to gather the harvest, or keep water out of the mines. No matter, the Cornish paid most of what was asked, for there was deep reverence for the king himself and for the English church, even though they had revolted against the introduction of the Church of England a hundred years before. Also, most Cornish followed the lead of Sir

Bevil Grenville, the most influential and best-loved man in the county. Sir Bevil was known for his generosity, adored by his servants and tenants, and as a loyal Royalist, represented Cornwall in 1640 in the *Long Parliament.* The long parliament could only be dissolved with the agreement of its members, and lasted from 1640 to 1648 when it was legally in abeyance, until recalled in 1659. It followed the *Short Parliament* that lasted just three-weeks.

At first, the Cornish parliamentarian representatives acted together, hoping for a compromise that limited the powers of the king. Loyalties divided however, when puritanical extremists and zealots, joined by those with consciences, failed to reach an agreement with those who supported the king. In the end, the glue that held the Cornish gentry together started to fracture, with some siding with parliament, and others siding with the king.

In 1641 all able men over the age of 16 in every parish in Cornwall had to sign the *Protestation Roll,* supporting King Charles I. Any in Lanreath who didn't sign would be at the least ostracised by every other villager, and certainly *threatened* by the very Royalist Grylls family who lived at Court Barton.

One hundred and seventy five men from Lanreath signed, putting the population at that time at an estimated four hundred and seventy five. These men would have been farm workers, miners, carpenters, blacksmiths, wheelwrights and other trades folk, but with war looming, they were recruited as soldiers for the king, and the Grylls family knew that their fortunes and prestige depended on the men of Lanreath putting up a good fight.

When the Civil War began, Bodmin and Truro declared for the king, while Sir Richard Buller from his headquarters at Saltash, declared for parliament and occupied Launceston. Across the Tamar, Plymouth sided with parliament. Liskeard stayed with the king, as did most other towns throughout Cornwall.

Sir Ralph Hopton, a loyal and experienced professional soldier marched from Truro with three thousand men raised in the West, and succeeded in taking the town of Launceston and Saltash from Sir Richard Buller, who was forced to withdraw to Plymouth. Thus, by the beginning of October 1642, all of Cornwall was in Royalist hands.

John Grylls from Lanreath was present at the siege of Launceston in his capacity as Sheriff, and rode around shouting that every man bearing arms against the king would be hanged. His men, no doubt including those from Lanreath, went in and proceeded to burn and loot the town, at which point he rode in to quell the riot.

With success in Cornwall, Hopton felt strong enough to take the offensive and advanced on Exeter, hoping to rally Devonshire men to the king's cause. This failed, forcing the Cornish army under Hopton to flee back to Cornwall. In the meantime, Saltash had been retaken by the parliamentarians based at Plymouth, and chasing Hopton's retreating army, took Liskeard as well, pushing the Cornish all the way back to Bodmin.

By a stroke of luck, three parliamentarian warships carrying arms and money had run aground off Falmouth. This booty was rushed to Sir Ralph Hopton and Sir Bevil Grenville who were camped in the grounds of Boconnoc on the 18th January 1643, with *Foot* (Infantry) and *Horse* (Cavalry). Boconnoc is between Liskeard and Bodmin, a short distance from Lanreath.

Falmouth estuary looking out from Pendennis castle

At the same time, the parliamentary garrison at Plymouth commanded by General Ruthin moved into Cornwall. Instead of waiting for an additional army led by the Earl of Stamford who was moving down from Somerset to join him, Ruthin decided to engage and win a victory for himself.

On breaking camp on the morning of 19th January, Hopkins and Grenville were surprised to learn that General Ruthin was camped just two miles away in front of the little church at Bradock. In high spirits with new weapons and money from the looted warships, and on their own turf, the Cornish army were ready to take the initiative. With 4,000 Foot and 500 Horse against the advance force of Ruthin with 4,000 soldiers, the two armies thus met on the picturesque ridge between Bradock and Boconnoc. This was the first battle of the Civil War in Cornwall, now known as *The Battle of Bradock Down*.

After prayers, the Royalists advanced, with Grenville leading the Foot in the centre, and Hopton the Horse on the flanks. It didn't

Bradock Down church   *Bradock Down battle ground*

last long, for so fierce were the Cornish in their charge, that the parliamentarian forces broke ranks at the first wave, and fled in total shock.

Within two hours, the Cornish had killed two hundred men and captured more than 1,200, with only a few losses themselves. John Grylls and his eldest son Charles from Court Barton would have played a major part in that battle, together with the 175 men from Lanreath.

When the battle was over, the Cornish soldiers were very sparing of shedding more blood, having a noble Christian respect for their brethren. Sir Ralph Hopton had puritanical ideals, and Sir Bevil Grenville had a leaning that way. The Grylls were Church of England – indeed, John Grylls's brother Francis was at that time the Rector of St Marnarch's church in Lanreath.

After the battle, Hopton went off to Saltash in pursuit of Ruthin. On the afternoon of 22nd January, Hopton attacked, driving through their defences, and pushing the garrison down the steep slope and into the Tamar river. Again, the Royalist losses were light, but many of the parliamentarian forces were killed, and many more drowned, leaving behind them twenty guns and a hundred prisoners.

In just four days, from Bradock Down to Saltash, the Cornish had achieved two astonishing victories with few losses, but with heavy losses to the parliamentarian forces. At the beginning of 1643, all of

Cornwall was back in Royalist hands.

In May of 1643, the Earl of Stamford with an army of 5,600 men had reached Cornwall, and took defensive positions on the summit of a substantial hill just outside Stratton, now called Stamford Hill. Sir Ralph Hopton, with a much smaller force of 3,000 Cornishmen, chose to attack this formidable position, taking advantage of the absence of parliamentary Horse, and fearing the arrival of another parliamentary force led by Sir George Chudleigh.

The hill that gave the Cornish their legendary status

Although being outnumbered by almost two to one, and against a better equipped, fed and prepared force, the Cornish under the overall command of Hopton, was tactically superior. The Cornish commanders included, Mohun, Grenville, Berkeley, Slanning and Trevanion. The Cornish forces advanced with the Foot, while the Horse covered the rear. Time and again they charged, fired, reloaded and charged again, advancing without pausing. Although Chudleigh arrived and led a counter-attack, the final flood tide of the Cornish Foot proved unstoppable, until at last they broke over the summit and the enemy fled. After ten hours of fighting, the Cornish Royalists had killed three hundred parliamentarians, captured 1,700 prisoners, including Chudleigh, as well as 13 artillery pieces, a mortar, substantial provisions and £5,000 in cash. More importantly, Hopton and his commanders had secured Cornwall with its valuable tin mines and ports for the Royalist cause. Chudleigh was so disheartened by Stamford's timid incapacity against Hopton's forces, and so full of admiration for the courage and

Godliness of the Cornish, who sang a *Te Deum* after their victory, that he changed his allegiance. *Te Deum laudamus: te Dominum confitemur. Te aeternum Patrem omnis terra veneratur* - "We praise Thee, O God: we acknowledge Thee to be the Lord. All the earth doth worship Thee and the Father everlasting."

Battle monument at Stratton

After the battle of Stratton, the Cornish Foot acquired an almost legendary reputation, not only because of their fighting qualities, but also because of their religious discipline, their chivalry and devotion to their commanders, such as Hopton and Grenville. Only their ancestors in Arthurian romance, who kept the Saxon invaders at bay for so long, matched this reputation.

At the end of May 1643, Hopton led a force of nearly four thousand Cornishmen to Chard in Somerset, where they were joined by the Royalist army under the Marquis of Hertford, and Prince Maurice with his Cavaliers. The joint force occupied Taunton and Bridgwater, then advanced on Bath.

The Cornish Foot, flushed with the success of Stratton, asked to be led up the heavily defended hill by their beloved Grenville. After a long battle, they reached the top, but the parliamentarian force withdrew under cover of darkness, and took up their final position within a walled enclosure. It was a hollow victory, as Grenville had been mortally wounded at the moment of victory and died the next day. The death of Grenville was irreparable for the Cornish, as it was for him they fought, and not some remote, unknown king. After the battle, Hopton was severely injured by an exploding ammunition wagon, and this further depressed the Cornish.

The parliamentary force in Bath was soon joined by forces from Bristol, and went on the offensive, catching up with the Royalist forces at Devizes. Low on ammunition after the wagon explosion, the Cornish were forced to make bullets out of lead taken from the roof of churches, and 'match' made from bed-cords (rope soaked in saltpeter used as the ignition for the matchlock musket). For three days the Cornish held out, gaining the respect of the parliamentarian leaders who recorded their bravery. Things changed in favour of the Cornish, when a Royalist force of Horse broke through from Oxford and attacked the parliamentarians head-on at Roundway Down. This enabled the Cornish Foot to attack the parliamentarians from the rear.

When Prince Rupert arrived from Oxford, their army was now nearly fifteen thousand men. The Bristol garrison was under two thousand men, although their defences were very strong, in particular on the south side where the Cornish were posted. Although the Cornish counselled a siege, Rupert facing weaker defences to the north favoured an assault, and so it was. Slanning and Sir Thomas Basset now led the Cornish. They attacked over a broad ditch before attempting to scale a high wall. After a three-hour assault, and with the loss of a third of their force, the Cornish withdrew. Prince Rupert however broke through the weaker defences, and five hundred Cornish Foot, although battle-weary from their defeat, answered the call and forced their way into the city centre. Only one Bristol fort was taken with the castle remaining intact. The parliamentary garrison marched out the next day, and left the city and port in the hands of the king.

The price the Cornish paid for victory was high. Of the three thousand that marched out of Launceston with Hopton and Grenville, only half now remained, and most of their leaders had gone – Godolphin, Grenville, Trevanion and Slanning, all now dead. All fought together, and all died together. "*Gone the four wheels of Charles' wain, Grenville, Godolphin, Trevanion, and Slanning, slain.*"

The Cornish refused to lay siege to Gloucester, preferring to march home under the new leadership of Prince Maurice leading the Foot, and the Earl of Carnarvon leading the Horse. Although the Cornish was now much less a fighting force than it was, their reputation was awesome. So much so, that as they marched through the West Country, town after town fell with scarcely a blow – Dorchester, Weymouth, Portland, Bideford and Barnstaple, with even Exeter on the point of capitulation. All heard the Cornish could *run up walls twenty feet high*.

Even the newly installed Sir Alexander Carew, who was in command of the Plymouth parliamentary garrison at Drake's Island in The Sound, lost his nerve and secretly offered to surrender to the king. After being betrayed by a house servant, he was caught, tried for treason and beheaded at Tower Hill. *"Dost thou hear,"* he said to the executioner, *"when I say; Lord, though thou killest me, yet will I put my trust in Thee, then do thou cut off my head."*

The king was so proud of his Cornish supporters, that he sent a *declaration unto all his loving subjects in the County of Cornwall*, thanking them for their extraordinary zeal, patience and courage in his cause. He ordered copies to be published in every church. A copy still exists in St

King Charles I monument in Whitehall

Marnarch's church to this day, close to the south door where it has hung for more than three and a half centuries.

At the beginning of 1644, Sir Richard Grenville, the younger brother of Sir Bevil, returned from the war in Ireland, and after securing his back-pay from parliament, accepted a commission as lieutenant-general to Sir William Wallert. This gave him access to military secrets, and shortly after, he switched sides and joined the king at Oxford. Although the Cornish were welcoming of another Grenville, Sir Richard was very different to his former brother, being brutal and cynical, albeit a fine soldier. The parliamentarians issued a proclamation against him for his treachery using several offensive epithets, one of which was skellum (scoundrel), and thereafter referred to him as *Skellum Grenville*.

Meanwhile, a parliamentarian force led by the 3rd Earl of Essex, Robert Devereux, having been led to believe by Lord John Robartes of Lanhydrock, then in Royalist hands, that he could expect substantial support from the people of Cornwall, crossed the Tamar on 26th July 1644. He then advanced through Liskeard to Lanhydrock and Bodmin. Robartes himself had not been to Cornwall for two years, and may have been misguided in his opinion by his steward, Tregagle.

On arrival, Essex found that instead of the friendly peasants he was told to expect, he was surrounded by a hostile people, aroused by

A Letter of Thanks to the inhabitants of Cornwall, from Sudely Castle on the tenth day of September 1643.

We are highly sensible of the extraordinary merit of our County of Cornwall, of their zeal for the defence of our Person, and the just rights of our Crown in a time when we could contribute so little to our own defence or to their assistance in a time when not only no reward appeared, but great and probable dangers were threatened to obedience and loyalty; of their great and eminent courage and patience in the indefatigable prosecution of their great work against so potent an enemy, backed with so strong, rich, and powerful cities, and plentifully furnished, and supplied with men, arms, money, ammunition, and provisions of all kinds; and of the wonderful success with which it hath pleased Almighty God, although with the loss of some eminent persons who shall never be forgotten by us, to reward their Loyalty and Patience by many strange Victories over their and our enemies, in despight of all human Probability, and all imaginable Disadvantages; that as we cannot be forgetful of so great Deserts, so we cannot but desire to publish to all the world, and perpetuate to all time, the memory of these their merits, and of our acceptance of them, and to that end, we do hereby render our Royal thanks to that our county in the most public and lasting manner we can devise, commanding copies hereof to be printed and published; and one of them to be read in every Church and Chapel therein, and to be kept for ever as a Record in the same, that as long as the History of these Times, and of this Nation shall continue, the Memory of how much that County hath merited from us, and our Crown, may be derived with it to posterity.

Given at our camp at Sudely Castle, the tenth of September, 1643

Transcription of letter from King Charles I as written

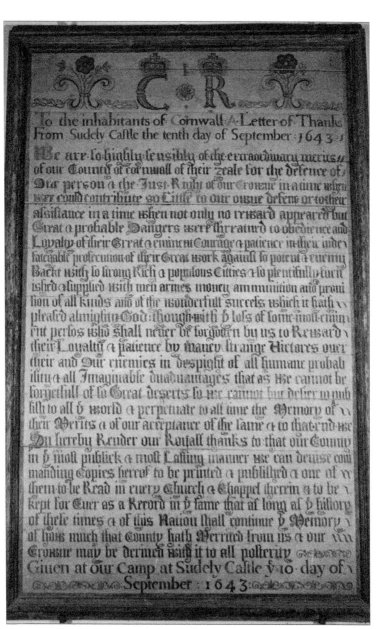

C R

To the inhabitants of Cornwall A Letter of Thankes
From Sudely Castle the tenth day of September 1643

We are so highly sensibly of the extraordinary merits
of our County of Cornwall of their zeale for the defence of
Our person & the Just Right of our Crowne in a time when
wee could contribute so Little to our owne defens or to their
assistance in a time when not only no reward appeared but
Great & probable Dangers were threatned to obedience and
Loyalty of their Great & eminent Courage & patience in their under
fatigable prosecution of their Great work against so potent a enemy
Backt with so strong Rich & populous Citties & so plentifully furn
ished & supplied with men armes money ammunition and provi
sion of all kinds and of the wonderfull success which it hath
pleased almighty God: Though with y loss of some most eminin
ent persos who shall never be forgotten by us to Reward
their Loyalty & patience by many strange Victores over
their and Our enemies in despight of all humane probab
ility & all Imaginable duaduantages that as We cannot be
forgetfull of so Great deserts so we cannot but desire to pub
lish to all y world & perpetuate to all time the Memory of
their Merits & of our acceptance of the same & to that end We
Du hereby Render our Rayall thanks to that our County
in y most publick & most Lasting manner we can devise com
manding copies hereof to be printed & published & one of
them to be Read in every Church & Chappel therein & to be
kept for Ever as a Record in y same that as long as y history
of these times & of this Nation shall continue y Memory
of how much that County hath Merited from us & our
Crowne may be derived with it to all posterity
Giuen at our Camp at Sudely Castle y 10 day of
September: 1643

Charles I letter displayed in St Marnarch's church, Lanreath his invasion, and with no chance of getting the supplies or the recruits he had expected. On learning that the Royalists at Launceston had closed off his rear, he withdrew to Lostwithiel at the end of the Fowey estuary. Earlier, the Earl had arranged to be re-supplied by ship from Portsmouth, but strong westerly winds had prevented the ships from leaving their home port.

In the meantime, the king having been reinforced, started to march on the parliamentary forces at the beginning of August – outnumbering them by two to one with four Royalist armies. This confined the parliamentarians to the Gribbin peninsula and the valley of the Fowey between Lostwithiel and the sea.

In Lostwithiel, less than six miles from Lanreath, the Roundheads with 10,000 men (7,000 Foot and 3,000 Horse), were in hostile surroundings, and forced to steal food from the 700 residents, and take over their homes while they waited to be supplied by sea. In an act of aggression, the Great Court at Lostwithiel was set on fire, a symbol of Cornish Royalism and Cornish independence. An attempt was also made to blow up the parish church with Royalist prisoners inside. Burn marks can still be seen in the tower to this day.

Former Lostwithiel jail   *Lostwithiel bridge*

The king, by contrast, ordered his troops to respect and not alienate the Cornish people, who he regarded as his own, as so many of them were tenants or workers on Duchy manors. Prince Maurice hanged at least one of his men for looting at Lanhydrock.

Grenville had taken Bodmin and was at Lanhydrock on the west bank of the river. King Charles and his troops stayed first at Liskeard, then at Boconnoc. Local tradition has it that he visited Lanreath, as their leader, John Grylls of Court Barton, was made Sir John in August 1644. It is known that the Kings Lifeguard of Horse was billeted in a field that was to become known as Soldiers Park. This 17 acre field is still part of the Court Barton estate, and includes cattle sheds, a milking parlour, and land behind. With no evidence that the king did indeed visit Lanreath, the story may have be fabricated by an enterprising landlady to increase trade. If so, the story stuck and is still believed today, much to the anger of some local historians.

With 10,000 parliament army men billeted at Lostwithiel and no supply ship arriving, and with no support from the Cornish people, the pillaged food of chickens, pigs and grain from the fields quickly ran out. Also, everything that happened in Lostwithiel would be reported to the king, and would have been the hot topic of conversation between the men of Lanreath, and the Grylls family. On the old roads, the Punch Bowl Inn was strategically between Liskeard and Bodinnick, where the ferry crosses to Fowey.

River estuary at Fowey   *Restormel castle*

On 13th August the king's troops attacked north of Lostwithiel, taking several outposts. On the 21st August Grenville took Restormel castle, putting Fowey under direct threat. General George Goring with three-thousand men, took St Austell and St Blasey, and the little port of Par, depriving Essex of the remaining waterfront from which to escape. When all food had run out for the Roundheads, the Earl of Essex on the night of the 30th August sent the remainder of his 3,000 Horse led by Sir William Balflour, through the Royalist lines to escape to Plymouth. In an effort to escape, the parliamentarian Foot tried to retreat to Fowey under cover of darkness and in pouring rain, but had to abandon several guns that got bogged down on the muddy roads along the way.

On the morning of the 31st they arrived at Castle Dore, and there they made their last stand within the ramparts of King Mark's former residence. All day they fought, the Cornish Foot leading the attack, and as darkness fell, they broke through the eastern gate, thus

69

cutting off the parliamentarian's line of retreat to Golant on the river Fowey a mile away - the gateway to the sea.

Early next morning, Essex and Robartes slipped away and sailed for Plymouth in a fishing boat, deserting Sir Philip Skippon, their Sergeant Major-General of Foot who, by now, was surrounded on all sides with little chance of escape. Although Skippon wanted to break out as the Horse had done, he was overruled and forced to accept the king's honourable terms of surrender.

Castle Dore

The wounded were to be sent by sea from Fowey to Plymouth, and the remaining 6,000 Foot were to be disarmed, and allowed to proceed by land under guard. The guard, however, did little to stop the anger of the Cornish peasants on their march to Plymouth. It's recorded: *"We were inhumanely dealt with, abused, reviled, scorned, torn, kicked and pillaged, many stripped of all they had, for even in the presence of the king and the general they took away our clothes, coats and hats."* Of those who survived to surrender, at least 300 per day lost their lives on the 30 mile trek, due to attacks, malnutrition, cold, disease and infected wounds. Eventually, just 1,000 reached the safety of Poole in Dorset. At last, the Cornish Celts avenged themselves on the invading Saxons.

Little is recorded of the battles that Sir John Grylls of Court Barton and the men of Lanreath fought in, except that of the siege of Launceston led by Sir Ralph Hopton at the start of the Civil War. As the Sheriff of Cornwall, his was the first name on a *Petition of Loyalty* sent to the king on 22nd May prior to war starting. 7,000 in total signed, and in it they asked the king "*Never to suffer your Subjects to be governed by an arbitrary government, nor admit any alteration in Religion*." Their main concern was "*To preserve the established Church from papist and Puritan attack*." Also as High Sheriff, John was involved in a Parliamentary dispute regarding the treatment of the people of Launceston, which had been taken by the Royalists, along with Saltash after the parliamentarians retreated without a fight. However, it can be safely assumed that John and his men from Lanreath were deeply involved in the fighting, under the overall command of Hopton, and also Grenville, or one or other of the major Royalist commanders.

Although the king's troops and the Cornish armies kept the Roundheads out of Cornwall, elsewhere in England the victories were with parliament. So in 1646 the Civil War ended and King Charles was put on trial and found guilty of treason. He was beheaded in 1649 and for 11 years England had no king or queen. This was a most humiliating time for Cornwall, the Cornish, and the people of Lanreath who fought for and supported the cause of King Charles I. The Grylls family were found guilty by parliament, with Sir John Grylls having to give up his land, with the rents going to government, and being given a hefty fine.

The Reverend Francis Grylls was ejected from his post as Rector, to be replaced by a government supporter. Although *not* recorded on the Rector's Roll in St Marnarch's church, it is known to be a person called John Bracegirdle, who was appointed as *an Intruder* on 4th June 1646. His Patron was given as *The Protector*, who was, of course, Oliver Cromwell.

In 1651 Sir John's son Charles Grylls finally paid a fine of £582, and things slowly started to return to normal. Francis Grylls was reinstated as Rector on the restoration of the Monarchy, when Charles II of the House of Stuart was crowned. Both Francis's son and grandson succeeded him as St Marnarch's church rectors.

It's not known if the Reverent Francis Grylls was involved in helping Royalist fugitives to escape, but it has been suggested that an underground tunnel, the entrance of which can still be seen in the old Rectory, may date from this period. A manhole cover hides the entrance from the current Rectory car park, which might have been hidden by straw inside of the former Coach House. There is a drop of six foot to the tunnel floor through a two foot square hole, then a thirty-foot long tunnel. At the end of the tunnel are two-rooms, one of which was used as the wine cellar, with the stone racks still in place.

On the 17th August 1660 Francis Grylls junior was installed as the Rector of Lanreath, staying in that post until his death 31 years later in 1691. Following his death, more of the Grylls dynasty became rectors, namely Nicholas and Richard, although a third, possibly in error, is listed as William Grylls.

The former 'hidden' stairs   *The 'secret' tunnel*

During Richard Grylls's incumbency, ecclesiastical records give a description of the Rectory. In addition to the *parlour with boarded floor*, there are said to be six rooms with plastered or partly plastered walls, one *handsomely,* and the hall is described as a *great hall, open to the roof.* The hall may have been much the same fifty years earlier, but by 1726, a great hall open to the roof was becoming more of a rarity and consequently would have been more likely to get a mention.

Richard Grylls seems to have taken a great interest in the garden and glebe land, planting a number of ash and sycamore saplings and growing apple trees in the pigeon house garden. He also had a high wall built around the vegetable garden, which lay on the western side of the house bordering the main village street. The southern part of this wall is still standing, although not now part of the Rectory. However, the three houses that now occupy the land are called Rectory Gardens.

The Rectory - east-facing view

A little later in the 18th century, the Grylls family established a rabbit warren to the south of Court Barton, which still exists today. The walls descend for half a metre or more below ground, and a metre and a half above - in effect, a free-range rabbit enclosure. The original capping had a slate course cantilevered inwards to prevent the rabbits escaping. The walls and the 105m x 65m ground is now grade-2 listed.

Charles Grylls, son of the late Sir John Grylls, settled into a quieter life at Court Barton with his wife Anna. He was himself

Rabbit warren wall with capping

made High Sheriff in 1662, and his son, also called Charles, became High Sheriff in 1700. One further generation on, the eldest son, yet another Charles Grylls, sold Court Barton to the Buller family of Morval in 1718.

The last of the Grylls family with connections to Lanreath was a young lady who was married in St Marnarch's church in 1766. Modern-day direct descendents of the Grylls dynasty still visit the village and give occasional historical talks at Court Barton, and Richard Grylls supplied much of the family information for this book.

73

As with Court Barton, the *famous* Punch Bowl Inn has a history that predates its current use as a pub from 1620. The assertion by the Punch Bowl Inn to be the very first licensed public house in the land, and a smuggler's den, thus giving it claim to the title famous, is difficult to prove. A photograph taken in 1951 shows a different inn sign, and a notice that reads: *"This is Lanreath. Historically interesting and famous for it's church, inn, maypole, and the setting of a well known film."* The film in question was made in 1947 and released a year later with the title "Daughter of Darkness." It starred the beautiful Anne Crawford, who died aged 35 after making 24 films, Maxwell Reed, the first husband of Joan Collins, and Siobhan McKenna, who went on to star as St Joan. It also featured Honor Blackman in her first film role, and later famous for the 1964 Bond film, playing *Pussy Galore*, and The Avengers. A local resident, then aged 12, recalls skipping church one Sunday to watch them filming sheep shearing in the grounds of Court Barton.

Built between about the 14th to 16th century, the Punch Bowl Inn would

Coach house entrance

Horse-mounting block - not original

originally have been used to accommodate travellers, including clerics and officials, and provide basic food and drink. Only later in 1620 did it convert into an inn to sell punch. The sign is typically pictorial from the 14th century used to identify its use in an illiterate age. The current sign, however, is a reproduction erected during the 1950s, possibly by a landlord called Idris Jenkins, or a later landlord. Signs for alehouses were not common until the 16th century.

The word *punch* comes from the Hindi word *panch*, meaning *five*, and consisted of alcohol, sugar, lemon, water and tea or spices. As sailors and employees of the British East Indian Company only introduced it into England in the early 17th century, the Punch Bowl Inn's claim to be the first licensed pub in England could be directly related to being allowed to serve and sell this new drink. The first *recorded* mention of *punch* however was in 1631, so as the Punch Bowl Inn's claim to have been licensed to sell it from 1620, leaves a discrepancy of eleven-years for which the jury is still out.

Current Punch Bowl Inn sign

Evidence that the Punch Bowl Inn was a coaching inn can be seen from the wide entrance from the road, leading through to the rear of the pub, and steps at the front to enable a rider to mount their horse, although the ones seen today are not original. The original building was said to include a blacksmith's working area in the basement, and if that were so, it would have been located down a flight of steps close to the present restaurant, through a doorway that still exists today, and into a courtyard. That courtyard has since had many changes, and is now a house with a bow-window. Having a blacksmith on the premises would have been a great asset to the original coaching inn.

The Punch Bowl Inn in 1951, with the Jenkins and William's families

During the Civil War in 1644, the king, accompanied by his fourteen year old son (the future King Charles II), his entourage and his generals, stayed first in Liskeard and then at the great mansion of Boconnoc, four miles north of Lanreath. As the siege went on the area between the Fowey and Looe Rivers must have teemed with Royalists troops. Some were definitely quartered in Lanreath in what is still called *Soldier's Park*. Some officers, it can be assumed, stayed in the building and many rooms currently owned by the Punch Bowl Inn.

Jonathan Trelawny, born in Pelynt into an old Cornish family, was ordained a priest in 1676 and in 1685 was appointed the Bishop of Bristol under King Charles II. When Catholic James II took the throne and issued the *Declaration of Indulgence* towards Catholics, seven bishops including Jonathan Trelawny were incarcerated in London. Most Cornishmen were furious and asked "*And Shall Trelawny Die*", but having given so much to the Royalist cause in the Civil War, the memory of the lives lost were still fresh in their minds. When the news came of Trelawny's acquittal of seditious libel, cheers were heard in Westminster Hall and on the streets of London. Church bells rang out in Bristol and fires were lit in many parts of the city. When the news reached Cornwall, the church bells rang out in Pelynt, and the Mayor of Looe ordered cannons to be fired.

This became a pivotal time in England, and soon afterwards William of Orange took the throne with the approval of the Church of England, James II fled the country, and Trelawny went on to become Bishop of Exeter and then Bishop of Winchester. The imprisonment of Trelawny gave rise to the *unofficial* Cornish anthem with the rousing chorus "*And shall Trelawny live, And shall Trelawny die, Here's twenty thousand Cornish men will know the reason why.*"

The words to the song were written in 1824 by an eccentric parson on the north Cornish coast called Robert Stephen Hawker, known for his work in rescuing and burying the remains of shipwreck victims washed up on the rocks below his church. Outrageously dressed in a claret-coloured coat, blue fisherman's jersey, long sea-boots and a pink brimless hat, he would often talk to birds. He also invited his nine cats into the church, then excommunicated one of them when it caught a mouse on a Sunday. It's probable Hawker based his song on a previous one, and exaggerated the events of 1688 in his lyrics.

'Trelawny' Lyrics - also called 'Song of the Western Men'

With a good sword and a trusty shield, A faithful heart and true
King James's men shall understand, What Cornish men can do
And have they fixed the where and when? And shall Trelawny die?
Here's twenty thousand Cornish men, Will know the reason why

And shall Trelawny live? Or shall Trelawny die?
Here's twenty thousand Cornish men, Will know the reason why

Out spake the captain brave and bold, A merry wight was he
Though London Tower were Michael's hold, We'll set Trelawny free
We'll cross the Tamar, land to land, The Severn is no stay
Then one and all and hand in hand, And who shall bid us nay

And shall Trelawny live? Or shall Trelawny die?
Here's twenty thousand Cornish men, Will know the reason why

And when we came to London wall, A pleasant sight to view
Come forth, come forth, ye cowards all, Here are better men than you
Trelawny, he's in keep in hold, Trelawny he may die
But twenty thousand Cornish men, Will know the reason why

And shall Trelawny live? Or shall Trelawny die?
Here's twenty thousand Cornish men, Will know the reason why

In the Victoria and Albert Museum, Bouronite, metallic *cog-wheel* twin crystals with quartz from the Herodsfoot mine are displayed. Also, crystals of Calcite, looking like white doves with their wings open can be seen, as well as Tetrahedrite.

It was the good fortune of Lanreath to have mines in the area, so much so that the neighbouring parish of Pelynt took it as a *geological insult* having no mines of their own. It may well be that this insult started the long rivalry between the two parishes, that still rumbles on to this day.

Bouronite

Calcite

Herodsfoot mine remains

Chapter Seven:

Georgian Period - AD 1714 to 1837

With the end of the Civil War, the execution of Charles I, and the Restoration of the Monarchy, the impoverished Cornish people took little interest in the events in England. Indeed, Cornwall was still barely accessible beyond the Tamar, and its people more interested in preserving their Celtic legends, festival and folklore, and even language in the far south-west.

Geologically, Cornwall had metals that the remainder of England didn't have, and the knowledge to mine tin, copper, lead and other metals and minerals. An adventurous, young, aristocratic and puritanical lady, Celia Fiennes, rode to Cornwall on horseback, crossing the Tamar at Cremyll Ferry. From there she passed Mount Edgcumbe and headed to Looe, then to Fowey, maybe passing through Lanreath, and onto St Austell. Although not recorded, the Punch Bowl Inn would have been a natural stopping over point. There she would have found accommodation, food, safe drink, stabling and an in-house blacksmith. Nicholas Grylls, the Rector of St Marnarch's church, and the Grylls family at Court Barton would have known of her visit, and no doubt put their political differences aside, knowing that her father was the parliamentarian defender at Bristol during the Civil War, to welcome her. Celia Fiennes recorded the life of tin miners around St Austell in great graphical detail, documenting the whole process the miners were using, as well as socio-cultural and socio-economic accounts. As graphic as the accounts of Celia Fiennes were, no words could describe the hardship suffered by those whose job it was to dig the actual tin and copper ore out of the ground. Descending to depths of 1,000ft or more, miners would clamber down slippery ladders, often with broken rungs, and with only a candle stuck to their hat for light, held on with nuggets of clay. Once at the bottom, they would have to crawl along a passageway to the tin seams, where they would chip away for between eight to twelve-hours in sweltering heat and little air. The isolation was enhanced by the fear of the *knackers* - mischievous elves who had to be appeased in order to keep you safe. As the Cornish folk song goes: "*Tom Trevorrow what have you done, You should have left the knackers a crumb, For they may bring the ceiling down, When next you venture underground.*"

On the surface, many miners' wives, or *bal maidens,* pounded the stone ore, and children from 12 years old, washed away the dust and light debris to leave the heavy tin ore. Home was a small isolated cob-built hovel with a cold, damp earthen floor and a thatched roof. Living under such conditions, temporary escape was often found by drinking gin or other spirits, then resorting to violence when hungry or angry.

This gave the Cornishmen the reputation of being little more than savages, and certainly during this time inter-parish warfare was rife and difficult, if not impossible, to control. In truth, the isolation of Cornwall gave more opportunities for lawless practices than the Anglo-Saxons the other side of the Tamar. With a coastline festooned with small secluded bays and a history of seafaring, some Cornishmen saw this as an opportunity. This included those from Lanreath no doubt, as the village lies just a few short miles from Talland Bay, Polperro, and the larger sea port of Looe. It was no wonder therefore, that any opportunity to make *something on the side* was viewed as a *gift from God.* Indeed, the thinking was that although it might be wrong to kill, it

Rugged coastline of Cornwall

was equally wrong to interfere with the *Will of God* and warn ships of any danger. A Parson Troutbeck is said to have prayed, *"Dear God, we pray not that wrecks should happen, but if it be Thy will that they do, we pray Thee let them be to the benefit of Thy poor people."*

The law at that time was that if a man or a beast escape from a shipwreck and reached shore, then it was not *legally* a wreck. But if all perished, it became the property of the coastal Lord of the Manor – although in practice, the property of whoever arrived first. So, on a stormy night, any ship close to the shoreline was followed with anticipation of it being wrecked, and those that were, were surely doomed. Any unfortunate sailor needing rescue was routinely ignored, and those who made it to the shore alive were quickly pushed back into the sea. Indeed, the sharp wrecking tools of axes and machetes were not only used for opening the cargo! The Cornish wreckers could clear the largest ships of their cargo within 24-hours – and had to do so before the government custom men arrived. In Georgian times, people had to pay huge taxes on luxury goods, brought in from abroad. So, brandy, gin, tea and salt could make a lot of money for smugglers, provided they didn't get caught, of course. If sheer poverty drove the tin miners to become night-time wreckers and smugglers, greed drove the Cornish gentry to organize its disappearance and sale, and pay off magistrates and excise men in brandy to turn a blind eye. For any excise men who tried to do their duty, going up against large numbers of drunken tinners lugging their booty to be hidden, inevitably ended up with fierce and bloody clashes, mutilation and murder. Lanreath men and others would pre-arrange to meet ships from France, the Channel Islands or the Scilly Isles, to off load their illegal hoard, and race it back to their village. Once back, the goods would be hidden in tunnels that ran under such places as the Rectory, the Punch Bowl Inn, and even the church, as some would believe. Over the years the well concealed entrances have mostly been lost, if they existed at all, but the one at the Rectory still exists with a *dropping zone*, tunnel, and two storage rooms.

There are many in Lanreath today who swear that tunnels exist under the Punch Bowl Inn and the church, and that the original Rectory tunnel extended to the Giant's Hedge, but no evidence has been shown or found by this author. One lady over 70 recalled to me that as a child of ten she was "*shown the entrance*" to a tunnel in the panelled room of Court Barton while playing with the owner's children. The current tenant still plays the same joke on today's visiting children by tapping the panels and getting them to listen to the hollow sound - "*That's the tunnel,*" they say. No doubt in another 60 years these children will be recalling the day they were shown the entrance to the smuggler's tunnel at Court Barton, so let not the truth spoil a good yarn.

It was at this time and during the incumbency of the Reverend Richard Grylls (1719-1736), that several parishioners of Lanreath were scared out of their wits by an apparition they saw while crossing Blackadown Moor. The location is about two miles out of the village on the southern slopes of Bury Down. In the year 1725 in which the story is set, the area was very bleak moorland. The sighting and descriptions were so similar, that soon the parishioners started to believe it was the spirit of a farmer who had lost his land after losing a fiercely fought lawsuit. The sightings were of a coachman dressed all in black, driving a carriage drawn by *headless horses* and making dreadful noises. The stories were so numerous and from such credible witnesses, the Reverend Grylls wrote to the Reverend Doidge of Talland Bay, who was well known for his powers of exorcism. The letter was delivered by the church Sexton, who was a respected man in the village, and although unschooled and not an eyewitness, had often been woken at night by the *rattle of wheels* on the street leading to the village. Two nights later, the two reverend gentlemen rode out from the Lanreath Rectory to Blackadown Moor.

The night was particularly dark with a howling wind, and for some hours they waited, but saw nothing. Finally, they gave up and said their farewells, with the Reverend Doidge saying he wanted to take a *short-cut* back to Killigarth Manor, Talland Bay, where he resided with his Patron, the Reverend Archdeacon Kendall. After a short distance, the Reverend Doidge's horse stopped and refused to go on, so thinking it must be a *sign from God*, allowed the horse to go where it wanted – at which point it galloped back to the place they had been waiting a short time earlier. On arrival, he saw the black-coated coachman, the coach, and the *headless horses*, just as described by Lanreath villagers. At the coachman's feet was the Reverend Grylls, face-down. Keeping his head, the Reverend Doidge started praying aloud, but before he could finish, the coachman shouted "*Doidge is come, I must be gone*", then jumped into his seat and drove off into the night. The Reverend Grylls' horse had galloped back to Lanreath, waking the villagers, who became so worried they set out to find their Rector. On arrival, they found the Reverend Grylls being propped-up by the Reverend Doidge, in shock and hardly able to speak. The trick had worked, the Reverend Grylls had been taken in, and the Reverend Doidge, in collusion with his black-coated associate coachman, managed again to transport another consignment of casks of brandy and wine to a secure location.

The story has some interesting twists and turns. As both rectors were close friends, why was the Sexton used as the messenger? One might conclude, therefore, that it was a *double-blind* against the Sexton and Lanreath villagers? Why did the Reverend Doidge reside with his Patron most of his life rather than his Rectory, and even when Archdeacon Kendall died, continued to live on with Kendall's son? From Blackadown Moor to Killigarth Manor the old road passed through Lanreath - there wasn't a short-cut? Part of the old road still exists today and is called *Rattle Street*. The Reverend Doidge continued his *remarkable* skills in exorcism until he died, aged 93 in 1746.

Over the years, much of the smuggling activities have been romanticized, giving rise to folk literature and songs. One by Rudyard Kipling - A Smuggler's Song.

If you wake at midnight, and hear a horse's feet, Don't go drawing back the blind, or looking in the street, Them that asks no questions, they isn't told a lie, Watch the wall, my darling, while the Gentlemen go by.

If you do as you've been told, likely there's a chance, You'll be give a dainty doll, all the way from France, With a cap of Valenciennes, and a velvet hood, A present from the Gentlemen, along o' being good.

Five and twenty ponies, trotting through the dark, Brandy for the Parson, baccy for the clerk, Laces for a lady, letters for a spy, Watch the wall my darling, while the Gentleman go by.

After the Reverend Richard Grylls, the post of Rector passed to Hele Trelwny, then Joshua Howell. Joshua came from Wales and was educated at Christ Church, Oxford. He first came to Cornwall as the Curate of Looe, then Vicar of Pelynt, then Vicar of Morval, then Rector of Lanreath until his death. At first he was badly-off financially, partly because of the difficulty of collecting tithes valued at £200 per year. However, he married Dunnett Haweis, heiress to property in central Cornwall. This property was sold and property in the Looe, Lanreath, Pelynt, and the Lansallos area purchased. It is thought he made improvement to the Rectory during his tenure. He had several children and died a wealthy man. The Reverend Howell was certainly well connected, and entertained his friends with abundant bottles of good quality wine. In June 1756 he was entertaining the Cornish Rector of Ludgvan and St Just, the famous geologist and naturalist, William Borlase, at his new Rectory. Afterwards they rode together along the length of the Giant's Hedge. In later years, scores of wine bottles with distinctive labels were ploughed up in the fields surrounding the Rectory. One can only but speculate whether they came from a French or Spanish galleon, wrecked off the shores of Talland Bay or Polperro. No doubt he had a good *working relationship* with his parishioners and duly looked after his flock well.

John Wesley   *John Wesley house, Trewint*

For many years a close watch was kept on the coast, and during this time a blind eye was often turned upon the smuggling trade. So bad was the reputation of Cornish folks involved with smuggling, and the illegal sale and consumption of brandy, that Christian preachers John Wesley and his brother Charles concluded that only God could change their lives.

So, in 1743 they journeyed to Cornwall and began to hold meetings and spread their message. Both John and Charles were Anglican clergymen, fired-up preachers calling sinners to repent. They preached mainly to poor Cornish tinners. Their doctrine was little different to their clergy colleagues, it's only that they *believed* in what they were preaching and openly criticized the establishment who ran the church. In retaliation, the Vicar of Illogan hired a churchwarden and a mob to chase the Wesleys out of their parish, and paid nine shillings out of the parochial funds in a victory celebration at the local alehouse. Also, other clergy incited violence, resulting in mobs savagely handling them, and destroying their preaching houses. Rumours were also spread about that the Wesleys supported the Jacobite Rebellion and the Pretender to the English throne, Bonnie Prince Charlie. However, although they did have strong political views and Jacobite connections, supporting the return of a Catholic House of Stuart against the House of Hanover, was not one the Anglican Wesleys would have encouraged.

William Borlase was very much against the Wesley brothers, and in his additional capacity as a Magistrate hounded them relentlessly. It is doubtful that either of the Wesley brothers preached in Lanreath, but John is known to have preached in Polperro. At first, Cornishmen threw stones and mud at the Wesley brothers. Charles Wesley visited Cornwall just five times, while John made 32 visits. Eventually, however, John won through and thousands went to hear him preach throughout Cornwall, including Liskeard, St Austell, Bodmin and Looe. Joshua Howell, the Rector of St Marnarch's church in Lanreath from 1740 to 1785, was most concerned about the activities of the evangelistic preachers, and noted more than once, "*Some parishioners are dissenters and meet in peoples' homes holding services.*" From this it might be assumed that John, or one of his associate preachers – the Reverent W. Shepherd, John Nelson or John Downes, did visit.

Gwennap Pit where John Wesley preached

A Wesleyan Methodist chapel was established in Lanreath village in 1786 and closed in 1990, during which time 46 marriages took place. Another chapel was located at Mount Pleasant on the Bodinnick Road.

The preaching of John Wesley denouncing sin with threats of hell-fire and damnation, must have brought untold terror to the simple-minded tinners and their families, but with hope of a better life thereafter through *instant* salvation. The effect was to make Cornwall a less barbarous place and reduce drunkenness, but took away from them a few enjoyable, harmless pleasures of life such as hurling, wrestling and the traditional gaiety of the Cornish. If some verses of the Charles Wesley hymns were sung today, such as "*The soul there restless, helpless, hopeless, lies; The body frying roars and roaring fries*" they would be met by howls of laughter and derision.

Piracy and smuggling still went on, but the converts were more inclined to save the lives of those who were shipwrecked, than push them back into the sea. St Marnarch's church at this time was using the *structured* Book of Common Prayer, but the Wesleyan chapels didn't have this restriction. One recorded prayer went; "*Dear Lord, last week we axed 'ee vur rain. And when 'ee axed vur rain, dear Lord, us wanted dapper little showers like. But, oh Lord, this is redikus.*"

In an age of religious intolerance, when protestant England feared the might of the Catholic church, many royalists were men of stature. Most Cornish families were the supporters of King Charles I during the Civil War, and keen to regain their power and land with the restoration of the Monarchy.

During the 18th and 19th century, men worked on farms as labourers and their wives and daughters went into service, working for farm owners, the church Rector or other gentry. Others were trades-folk, such as carpenters, blacksmiths or leather workers. Many were poor and destitute, and the church did its best to limit the numbers starving or going into poor-houses. Even rectors were sometimes reduced to ending up in poverty on retirement, and church records show that some incoming rectors were required to pay former rectors an annual sum to save them from starvation.

Ordinary people who came to live in Lanreath that weren't *born* in the parish were treated as outsiders. Many who came to the notice of the church as being possible *Illegal Residents* had to prove their case, and if not proven, they were ejected and returned back to the parish to which they were born.

Many Lanreath residents worked in the silver, lead and iron mines at Herodsfoot and Botelet, or factories supplying materials. Mining was a dangerous business and in some areas, a fifth of the miners were killed in accidents. On one day in 1876 three Lanreath residents died from an explosion at a gunpowder factory in Herodsfoot, aged 26, 36 and 46 respectively. Census and church records show many also died from illnesses and accidents, and sadly many children, including Julie Agnes Kitson (ref. 16), who was the Rector's daughter.

Selection from church records - those who died from illness

1. Frances Hickson - died of scarlet fever aged 3 in 1837
2. Honor Keast - died of dropsey aged 47 in 1837
3. Susan Pointer - died of inflamation aged 4 in 1837
4. Jane Bullur - died of malignant sore throat aged 3 in 1838
5. James Tums - died of fits aged 2 in 1838
6. Caroline Olver - died of measles in aged 2 in 1838
7. John Marshed - died of a burst blood vessel aged 22 in 1840
8. Ann Frether - died of of thyphus (from fear) aged 75 in 1840
9. Mary Rundle - died a neglected child aged 11 in 1840
10. Elizabeth Couch - died of bowel inflamation aged 7 in 1841
11. Ann Frathey - died of whooping cough aged 1 in 1843
12. Grace Gilbert - died of paralasis aged 66 in 1848
13. Mary Couch - died of asthma aged 60 in 1851
14. James Oliver - died of paralysis aged 56 in 1852
15. John Basset - died of exposure in Crimea aged 33 in 1855
16. Elizabeth Edwards - died of diptheria aged 5 in 1863

Selection from church records - those who died from accidents

1. Jennifer Williams - died from old wound aged 69 in 1831
2. Jane Parasons - decline from accident - aged 28 in 1832
3. Ann Sowden - stick through eye into brain - aged 1 in 1833
4. Edward Tuchel, fell from rick - aged 41 in 1834
5. William Searle, gutter fell on him - aged 58 in 1835
6. James Martin, killed by falling wall - aged 31 in 1842
7. Moses Haris, injuries from cart upsetting - aged 20 in 1846
8. Francis Hicks, fall from horse - aged 40 in 1846
9. Philippa West, poisonous berries - aged 7 in 1849
10. Mary Pointer, burnt - aged 1 1853
11. Thomas Hailey, cart upset - aged 12 in 1853
12. John Hockings - accidental gun accident aged ? in 1856
13. Louisa Hill-Tumour, died falling from horse - aged 58 in 1870
14. Mary Ford, drowned - aged 2 in 1876
15. William Lemon, expolsion from gunpowder - aged 26 in 1876
16. (Julie) Agnes Kitson, fell from cart - aged 4 in 1884

Many folk stories are told of the Punch Bowl Inn. The most frequent is the tale of a demonic black cockerel believed to have been the angry soul of an old rector of the parish, who fell to his death down the stairs to the cellar whilst fetching a bottle of wine. His guest for dinner that night was a handsome young curate who had fallen in love with the rector's young and beautiful wife. After one bottle of wine was finished, the rector got up and proceeded to the wine cellar to fetch another. What happened then is still a mystery. Did he fall or was he pushed? We will never know. The very next day, according to the tale, a large black cockerel appeared and began attacking everyone in sight. Eventually the bird flew in through the window of the Punch Bowl Inn and straight into an old earthenware oven. A quick thinking kitchen maid imprisoned it inside, and a mason was duly called to cement it up for all eternity.

Stairs to house from cellar   *Wine racks in cellar*

As with many folk tales, there may be a thin thread of truth running through the story, although this author has failed to unravel it fully. However, it could relate to the Reverend Richard Buller, who at 87 employed a curate, and was being looked after by his unmarried granddaughter (confirmed from church records) after his wife died. The 'steep steps' above ran into the wine cellar of his rectory. Although he died while still at the rectory, church records failed to record his death as the law demanded - could it be then, that residents believed he lived on imprisoned in the oven of the pub?

The sealed-up Punch Bowl oven

It's hard to believe that a young curate would deliberately push his rector down the stairs, but as the rector loved his wine, and one bottle had already been consumed, slipping on the steep steps is not beyond belief. His first-born son, Alexander was a naval officer, and it was his daughter Alice who lived with her grandfather at the rectory, as well as the curate. Rumours of an affair must therefore have been buzzing around at the Punch Bowl Inn as, while Alice was looking after her grandfather, any affair would have to stay secret and it would have been unthinkable to marry - at least while the rector was still alive.

While this is just *wild speculation,* a murder did take place in Lanreath. So the story goes, William Achym of Pelynt sent his steward

to renew a lease on some property which he held under the Duchy, but the steward renewed the lease in the name of Buller, a rival landowner. In a rage, William chased his steward to the slopes of Blackadown Moor, and killed him on the spot at a place now called *Slew Gate.*

Slew Gate, Bury Down

Lanreath school children - date of photograph above unknown

Lanreath school and children taken the year it closed - 2007

Chapter Eight:

Victorian Period - AD 1837 to 1901

As the Georgian period was coming to an end, the new century brought an old established family from Pelynt into Lanreath – the Bullers. One of their sons was an Admiral, and *Buller's Quay* in Looe was named after him. The new rector was Richard Buller, and during his 26 years incumbency the Napoleonic Wars came to an end. In 1837 Victoria became queen, bringing in what was to be an important era in England. A second Richard Buller became rector in Lanreath at the age of 33, accompanied by his wife Elizabeth and two children.

One of the first things the second Richard Buller did in 1829 was establish and fund the original Lanreath School in the study of his rectory. The population of the village at that time was about 650. Fifty four of the day-children were enrolled for free, and six were paid for by their own parents. Six children also attended the school in the evening for free, and with the two children of Richard and Elizabeth Buller, the total number being educated in Lanreath was 68. Later, the school moved to a building in the corner of the gardens of the rectory, bordering the road. The schoolroom measured 4 x 8 metres, the lower wall in local stone, the rest of cob with two sheltered windows on either side of a door to give access to the village street. This existed until a new school was built in 1868 on Glebe land on the outskirts of the village, at the cost of £301.3s.2d. This purpose-built school educated generations of residents until 2007 when it sadly closed.

The Bullers were wealthy with excellent connections, and as they planned to do a lot of entertaining, embarked on elaborate alterations to The Rectory, finally adding a southern section that almost doubled the size of the house. The later extension formed the separate master and mistresses bedroom, and a first floor study or dressing room - now the living room of the Fowey apartment. The living room and bedrooms of the Daymer apartment were added, and on the ground floor, a large handsome drawing room and dining room, which now form a large part of the owners apartment. The thickness of the walls by the entrance to each room testifies to the strength of these walls. The Rectory building now contains something like twenty five rooms. Although the Victorian age had begun, the character of the building was Georgian. A portico added to the west front to create a harmonious whole has since been taken down and now forms the entrance hall and part of the kitchen. The gardens were also upgraded, and as a finishing touch, a large circular driveway entrance was built, but that land is now a bungalow with an upper living area just beyond the current driveway. When everything was complete, the Buller family had increased to seven children and so employed half a dozen servants, a nurse, and later a governess. Looking through the census records at this time, copies of which can be found in St Marnarch's church, one can find a lot of Lanreath residents in service.

The childrens' bedrooms now form the two bedrooms of the apartment called Epphaven and the nurse or governess would have used what is now the bedroom of Gorran Apartment.

Richard Buller was Rector for 54 years, making him 87 when he died in 1883, and when looking back over his life, it must have given him great satisfaction, and the residents of Lanreath much to talk about and celebrate with his growing family. Some of the original children to be educated by him would have been close to 50 years old when he died. John Buller-Kitson followed, and saw out the end of the Victorian era and the start of the First World War.

Painting by Ida Pollock of The Rectory with the circular driveway

During the time of John Buller-Kitson, local resident Richard Harris moved from a cottage in the village to a cottage near the church and established the first Post Office in Lanreath in 1895. On retirement at 87 years old, his son John took over in 1939, moved the Post Office to a cottage further up the road and ran that until he retired in 1960, passing the job of sub-postmaster to his daughter Joyce. Joyce and her husband moved the post office again and ran it until 1981 from the cottage that Richard Harris moved from in 1895. In a room next to the first Post Office was a cobbler's shop, run by Richard who made shoes to order, and later shoe repairs. His son John also did some cobbling, along with being the local taxi driver, leaving his wife to run the Post Office. The Post Office had its first telephone early in the century, but not until the 1930s was a public one installed. At the beginning of the service the Post Office only sold stamps for letters at one penny. Then telegrams were sold from 1906, and National Health payouts in 1911 introduced by the Liberal government of David Lloyd George. Next came billeting payments for evacuees, aerogrammes and letters for servicemen.

The final location of the Lanreath Post Office was Rowan Lodge, which closed in 2006. The residents then secured funds to purchase and convert the village public toilets into a shop and Post Office. Today, the Post Office deals with a raft of government requirements and the community shop has become the hub of village life.

Shop postcard showing past and present post office locations

Remembering the Lanreath lads who served during WW1

Lanreath Home Guard (WW2) – outside The Rectory

Back Row Left to Right: *Billy Mitch; William Pollard; Nicholas Penrose; Lewis Knight; Ken Sandy; Martin West; Sidney Stephens; Joe Olliver; Sidney Jeffery; George Martin; Norman Giles*

Second Row: *Reg Hawke; Wesley Yeo; Fred Woolcock; Victor Libby; Arthur Matthews; William Lamerton; Tom Mitchell; Arthur Tamblyn; Peter Tamblyn; Ernest Haley; Dennis Bunney*

Third Row: *Jack Mitchell; Joe Martin; Edmond Facey; ? Snell; Arthur Libby; Peter Haley; Jack Olliver; Roy Lang; Harry Tamblyn; Fred Jago; William Ruby; David Bunney; Tom Facey; Claud Frethey (Blacksmith)*

Front Row: *Wilfred Shepherd; Reuben Haley; Edgar Sandy; Harry Yeo; Martin Bunney; Rev. Charles Girling; Army Sergeant Major; Tom Mitchell; Stan Shepherd; William Haley; Jim Collings; Percy Libby; Les Wills*

Chapter Nine:

Modern Times - AD 1902 to 2015

John Buller-Kitson was the Rector from 1883, and during his tenure came the start of the First World War. Many men from Lanreath were called for duty, and many lost their lives. Their sacrifice is recorded on the war memorial outside the front of St Marnarch's church, and inside, some being brothers and cousins as their names will testify.

Just after the First World War ended, a group of Lanreath men acquired an army hut for use as a village hall, dismantled it, and erected it on the land that is now the Village Green. A year or two later a kitchen and billiard room were added, and twice weekly the hut was used as a doctor's surgery, utilising the ladies' cloakroom.

At the start of the Second World War, Charles Girling was rector and resided at The Rectory. One of his first acts was ordering the digging up of the west lawn to create a large emergency vegetable garden. Three houses now occupy the land, aptly called Rectory Gardens. Charles Girling, like many clergy throughout Cornwall, coordinated home guard activities during the war. The home guard of up to seventy men met regularly once a week in The Rectory to get their orders. Their

Remembering World Wars

weapons were stored in a cupboard in his study - a large area that has since been turned into the kitchen of the Caerhay's apartment. Some of the Lanreath home guard were assigned to protect the railway viaducts at Largin, and another at what is now Trago Mills, others to the church tower of St Marnarch's, and yet others to Bury Down. All the cross roads in the area were guarded. Most of the men were farmers during the day, then on home guard duty at night. In addition, the RAF had men assigned at strategic crossroads and on Bury Down with searchlights. Many young men of Lanreath village were called to

95

arms and fought overseas, and severn who died are remembered in St Marnarch's church. The adjoining parish of Herodsfoot however, was the only village in Cornwall not to lose a single person in the First or Second World Wars.

For over 178 years the school had seen many changes, not least being during the Second World War when 50 children from Camberwell in London were evacuated to Lanreath, doubling the numbers that needed schooling. Later, children came from Bristol and Plymouth. To accommodate all the additional children, the school held lessons at The Rectory as well as the Wesleyan chapel, and had additional teachers from London. Children were billeted with families throughout the parish. As the school had its history in the church, it's not surprising that religious education was part of the curriculum, but the school kept up a high level of education academically, socially and in the arts. Skipping and musical games were very popular, especially with the girls, including *Oranges and Lemons*, *Nuts in May*, *The Big Ship Sails Though the Alley, Alley-oh*, and *Blue Bells, Cockle Shells*.

During the war up to 40 German prisoners from a camp near St Austell, were driven on the back of a lorry by a Sergeant Onions to work on Lanreath farms each day, then collected at night. Farm owners were required to fill in forms to assess how good the prisoners were. A few were coded "*NBG*" by Lanreath farmers, making sure they didn't return. Most proved good workers however, and some were even live-in prisoners and remembered with affection, making toys for the children at Christmas time. One prisoner, Herbie Kastelan never returned to Germany after the war, but married the daughter of a Lanreath farmer who he met at a dance held at the former Lanreath school. At the end of the war things weren't too good for Herbie, and he was even banned from going into the Punch Bowl Inn. One day in front of others, a Mr Tambyln, who came from an old and established Lanreath family, came out of the pub with a pint glass in hand and gave

Herbie Kastelan in 2012

it to Herbie, who thereafter became a welcome resident in the village, He lived on in Lanreath with his wife until he died in October 2014.

Just before the war, new roads replaced the dirt lanes in Lanreath, with roads being lined with large stones, then covered with tarmac. During the war, American soldiers were billeted in the area and arms dumps hidden along the Lanreath-Bodinnick road, accessed through camouflaged holes in the hedgerows. As D-Day approached, the American troops collected all the ammunition under cover of darkness and loaded it onto boats at Bodinnick in the Fowey estuary, and quietly slipped away.

After the Second World War it became increasingly evident that The Rectory, built to house a self-sufficient community, no longer fitted into the modern world. After Charles Girling died in 1962, the church sold it off to a private company for conversion into eights flats. A new rectory was built on Richard Buller's orchard, and the remaining extensive land sold off as potential building sites. Inside The Rectory several rooms were partitioned, and the great central stairway taken away to make room for the kitchens and bathrooms of Fowey and Daymer apartments.

Old photograph of Lanreath

With new roads came buses that took the residents of Lanreath to other villages, towns and cities, and brought in tourists from far and wide. The bus from Pelynt to Liskeard proved invaluable for Lanreath farmers, who shot dozens of rabbits and transported them on market days to Liskeard. The poor houses became a thing of the past, as social benefits kept people out of poverty, and better health services were introduced. Access to dental and hospital care came to Lanreath, as did improved communication such as the telephone. The first private phone lines had to be shared with other families, so when picking up the phone, one sometimes heard neighbours talking to their family or friends! The old oil and gas lamps went as electricity came to Lanreath in 1953. Pipes that took water to every property in the village replaced the two hand pumps in Lanreath that had supplied water to the villagers and their animals over the years. Rubbish collection started when plastics and food packaging made that necessary, where previously most rubbish was recycled, or had to be burned or buried. Even with all this modernization, the population of Lanreath declined. Farm sizes increased, but due to modern machinery, fewer jobs were available for farm hands.

With the war over, former activities in Lanreath were revived, not least being Maypole dancing. So intense was the rivalry between competing villages to get the highest Maypole, that at times police intervention was necessary. Each year, a tree was selected in secret from nearby commercial woodlands, then illegally cut and carried back at night to Lanreath, where it was guarded around the clock. When having one maypole stolen by the rival Pelynt village, Lanreath villagers retaliated by not only stealing it back, but shooting out the tyres of the vehicle that was used to steal it.

The government encouraged the building of houses after the war, and farm land in Lanreath was sold off for a housing development – aptly called Grylls Park in remembrance to the family that were so influential for over 100 years. Some old farm workers' cottages were restored for residential use, and other cottages for letting to tourists.

The old pump outside Well Cottage is original, and the notice a replica of the original. This well has never run dry.

Well Cottage village water pump   *Top village pump*

The Corner Cottage might well pre-date the Punch Bowl Inn and be the site of the original guest dwelling for visiting pilgrims. The local monk would have lived in his mud hut with a thatched roof, and would not have had enough room to accommodate guests. The enterprising owner of the Corner Cottage, which may have been the church, would have thus offered accommodation and sustenance, and served homemade ale. Over time, more buildings would have been added as required for accommodation and services. The Old Shop was assumed to be the location of the blacksmith's yard, and still has a blocked off door to the Punch Bowl Inn's cellar.

A second Lanreath pub was called The White Horse and located behind Samuel's Cottage. Samuel's Cottage was a former brewery, now converted, but many of the former features still remain, like the front door that is wide enough to roll a beer barrel through.

Many up-market houses were built post-war, mainly on Glebe land sold off by the church. In 1986 a new village hall was built, replacing the one that stood on the village green. To celebrate the new millennium, a new building was erected on the green.

Sadly, in 2007, the village school that had educated generations of Lanreath children, closed, the land sold off and luxury houses built.

In 1986 St Marnarch's church roof was replaced. For future generations to find, a time-capsule was placed in the roof.

At the time of the Queen's Diamond Jubilee the village shop and Post Office, opened by the co-founder of the Eden Project Tim Smit in February 2007, has gone from strength to strength and is financially sound. Staffed mainly by volunteers, it stocks a raft of supplies, and is a convenient meeting point for residents and visiters alike.

Opening of shop and post office by Tim Smit

Well Cottage　　　　　*Village centre cottages*

Lanreath is popular with the press and TV as a progressive village that punches well above its weight. In 2007 BBC Two made a one hour programme on Lanreath called *Power to the People*. Many activities take place in the village, with the Lanreath Amenites Group taking a leading role. In 2011 the group won the Queen's Award for Voluntary Service in Cornwall, equivalent to an MBE.

Poster displayed to honour the Lanreath Amenities Group

Lanreath village centre with green and Millennium building

No historical survey has been done on the Lanreath village cottages, but it is thought that after the mud and wattle hovel put up by the first visiting saint on the current St Marnarch's church site, the Corner Cottage would be the location for visiting pilgrims to rest, then buildings added to the north and west following the original dirt roads.

Corner Cottage - maybe the location of the saint's guest house

Samuel's Cottage - the former brewery

101

Montage of photographs of St Marnarch's church

Chapter Ten:

Lanreath Today - 2015

Lanreath is a lovely village with many residents whose families go back generations, as well as residents who moved in from elsewhere. Everyone gets on well together and visitors are always made welcome.

A visit to St Marnarch's church is a must for any tourist – the things to look for in the Church are:

St Marnach's church, Lanreath

1. *War Memorial - sited at the church entrance*
2. *Former north entrance - to let the devil out at christenings*
3. *Tower door - this is normally locked*
4. *Sundial above the south door is dated 1828*
5. *Two corbels and the niche that would have held idols*
6. *Seven-legged parish stocks inside of the south porch*
7. *Norman Font at the back of the church*
8. *15th century wagon roof with finely-carved bosses*
9. *Hatchment - armorial diamond-shaped funeral shield*
10. *Restored plaque with Prince of Wales feathers*
11. *Pulpit - believed to be Elizabethan*
12. *Clergy stalls - rebuilt in 1911*
13. *North Transept (door locked), staircase to rood gallery*
14. *Jacobean chair (1610) donated by the Grylls family*
15. *Rood screen - spanning to Chancel and south side*
16. *13 painted rood screen panels - the best in Cornwall*
17. *Grylls monument - wood made to look like stone. 1623*
18. *The Lord's Prayer painted on a board*
19. *The Ten Commandments, also on boards*
20. *Lady Chapel/Grylls aisle, with Grylls pews and shields*
21. *Norman stone altar on the window ledge close to door*
22. *Piscina cut into the wall to drain the communian win*
23. *Thomas Dandy - gravestone badly worn and defaced*
24. *Copy of King Charles I letter to Cornish churches*
25. *Coat of Arms of King Charles II on restoration*

A full guide and history of St Marnarch's by Rosemary Pollock can be found at the Church entrance priced at £1.50

After a walk around the church with all its history, where better to head to than a pint of ale and a meal from the Punch Bowl Inn, which at the time of writing (February 2015) is closed.

> ### The Famous Punch Bowl Inn
>
> 1. The wide doorway of the former 'coaching inn'
> 2. Outside steps for mounting and dismounting your horse
> 3. The plaque giving the date of the original licence as 1620
>
> **The Punch Bowl Inn dramatically closed in May 2012 after almost 400-years serving the village as a pub. It is unknown if it will ever open again.**

Strolling back across the Village Green, be sure to visit the Lanreath shop and Post Office. Run mainly by volunteers, this busy little shop sells an array of foodstuffs, newspapers and ice cream, as well as local Lanreath postcards and sweets. Give yourself plenty of time however, as this is the place to chat and meet the locals.

> ### The Lanreath village shop and Post Office
>
> 1. Successfully run by the village folk since February 2007
> 2. Support our shop and buy our goods and supplies
> 3. Feel free to chat - we love meeting our village guests

The Rectory has always been the centre of historical Lanreath, and today offers comfortable tourist accommodation. This imposing building with its former circle driveway had gardens stretching to the main road on the west and south side, and as far down as the Tithe Barn. Even today some historical features can be seen, and most of the bedrooms have a pedigree that goes back a long time.

> ### The Rectory - offering self-catering accommodation
>
> 1. Each apartment has an interesting history
> 2. Home of Lanreath rectors for hundreds of years
> 3. Just a few moments walk to the shop and Post Office
> 4. Excellent accommodation for visitors
> 5. Family-run business

Lanreath Village Hall is the hub of community life, with its very active Rally Social Club, Football Club and amenity hall where many events take place throughout the year.

Lanreath Village Hall and Rally Social Club

1. *Available for rent for functions, and includes a kitchen*
2. *Residents are yearly members, and allowed ad-hoc guests*
3. *Visitors and tourist can join on a weekly or monthly basis*

From the village hall, it takes but a moment to walk to the Giant's Hedge. The best place to see it is to cross the road opposite the village hall, and proceed down the narrow road for 60 yards. The road cuts through the hedge, so it can be seen from both sides. The steep side and the width of the top clearly gives credence to the claim of it being an ancient defence structure. It's possible to walk alongside the hedge taking a left turn, but can be difficult as the pathway is badly rutted in parts and muddy in others. The Giant's Hedge crosses a number of parishes, and the general agreement is that it was built post Roman for defensive purposes, maybe against rival tribal lords, or cattle rustling, or a combination of reasons. Although some, including the well-respected historian William Borlase, believed it to be Roman, there is no evidence to support this theory.

As Bury Down lies on private land, it is unwise to visit and trespass. However, it can be clearly seen from the top road in Lanreath village, and at various points on the B3359. A public footpath from a nearby lay-by exists and goes close, but this is farmland and extreme care is necessary to protect the environment and animals.

Just inside the porch of the church are some old stocks, a relic of the past. Look up and one can see the sundial, as accurate now as when it was installed. The other end of the church is the North door, opened in the past for christenings to 'let the devil out.'

The well inset into Well Cottage lies just across from the church. Take photographs by all means, but remember that this is a private house.

On the right, up the village and past the pub is another water pump. Both pumps served the village for all their water needs until the end of the Second World War.

The Tithe Cottage and barn are very photogenic and it isn't hard to imagine what they looked like at the turn of the century when the garden extended to include what is now Rowan Lodge.

The current Post Office is the fifth in the village, the first being the cottage with its bow window. Two are located up the road, one on the left and one on the right called the Old Post Office. The last was Rowan Lodge. All now are private houses.

We have come to the end in our historic journey of the history of Lanreath. From Bronze to Iron Age people, from Celtic British to Anglo-Saxon then English. From more or less free communities to the authority of the Manor, serf to husbandman under the lordship of the

Grylls, Trelawney and Buller dynasties, farm tenant to farm owner.

I hope you have enjoyed our historic travel through time, and when you stand in the centre of our village looking out over to Court Barton, The Rectory, St Marnarch's church and the Punch Bowl Inn, reflect for a while on all that has passed before, and ponder what our future descendants will say and write about us.

The year 2012 will long be remembered in Lanreath, as the year the Olympic Torch passed close by in Liskard town, and the village celebrated the Queen's Diamond Jubilee.

Index

Lightning Source UK Ltd.
Milton Keynes UK
UKOW07f1245240716

279088UK00010B/29/P